RHONDDA BOROUGH LIBRARIES

CHILDREN'S DEPARTMENT

1. This book must be returned within 3 weeks of the date of issue, but you may renew the loan if no one else wants the book.

2. A charge will be made for overdue books.

3. Please report any lost or damaged books—a charge is usually made.

4. You may join at **one** Library, but your tickets can be used at any library.

5. Please let the Librarian know if you change your address.

SUSAN SCOTT, F.L.A.,
Borough Librarian

7000865028

Rhondda-Cynon-Taff County Borough Libraries
Llyfrgelloedd Bwrdeistref Sirol Rhondda-Cynon-Taf

School Library Service

If this book is found, please return it to the Schools Services Librarian, Mountain Ash Library.

Class __JF____COL____

No. _____

Julie Jones
County Borough Librarian

PAPER FLAGS AND PENNY ICES

Roger Collinson

Illustrated by Tony Ross

Andersen Press

For
Ethel, Alf and Win

First published in 1984 by
Andersen Press Ltd.,
19-21 Conway Street,
London W.1.

All rights reserved. No part of this publication may be
reproduced, stored in a retrieval system, or transmitted in
any form or by any means, mechanical, photocopying,
recording or otherwise, without the written permission of the
publisher.

©Text 1984 by Roger Collinson
©Illustrations 1984 by Andersen Press Ltd.

British Library Cataloguing in Publication Data
Collinson, Roger
 Paper flags and penny ices.—(Andersen
 young readers' library)
 I. Title II. Ross, Tony
 823'.914[J] PZ7

ISBN 0-86264-086-5

Printed and bound in Great Britain
by Anchor Brendon Ltd., Tiptree, Essex.

Chapter I

'Stop it, Minnie!... D'you hear? You'll 'ave Mum in in a minute, and then you won't 'alf get what-for.'

'Practising me swimming, ain't I?'

'Not 'ere, you ain't. If you don't wake Mum and Dad up, you'll go and tear the sheets or something.'

''Ere – watch me, Florrie. Am I doing it proper?'

'You're 'urting my bad ankle! Get off it, can't you?'

The bed springs squeak as Minnie threshes arms and legs; and, from his coronation picture on the mantelpiece, King George V looks sternly down.

Charlie yawns, blinking at the sunshine that slips between the curtains dragged across the Buckles' second bedroom window. Half asleep, he sprawls in the sagging mattress and listens to Bert still snoring there beside him.

'Blimey!'

Charlie speaks aloud and sits bolt upright. All his dreaminess has vanished on the instant.

''Ere, Bert, wake up!... Bert!' he calls, as Bert sinks down and settles in the hollow where Charlie has been lying.

'Wot?' Bert grumbles. 'Wasser matter?'

'It's *today*!... You know!'

'Wot?... I ain't late for work, am I?'

'No!' cries Charlie. 'It's Bank 'Oliday, innit... Bank 'Oliday! And we're going to Southend!'

Bert sighs.

'Oh, yerse,' he says. 'And what's the weather doing?'

Charlie throws the clothes back and scampers to the window, where he pulls aside the faded curtains and cranes his neck.

'S'all blue,' he reports. 'No clouds nor nuffin.'

'Could change,' Bert warns. 'S'early yet. Could easy turn out like yesterday. And the seaside ain't much fun in pouring rain... 'specially with kids.'

'Aw, shut up!' Charlie pleads, and searches the sky again. No, it's going to be a perfect day. It's got to be.

And now he picks up the rod, packed ready in its case, and holds it proudly, imagining the arching bamboo cane and clicking reel as he pulls his first fish from the waves. Not for a moment does he doubt fish will be caught. With a rod as fine as this, how can he fail? After all, old Mr Culley has caught hundreds with it.

Next door, in the girls' room, Minnie grows more reckless.

'I'm gonna do a dive,' she says, and struggles to her feet. 'Now – *one* to get ready – *two* to get steady – '

'Minnie, stoppit!'

'. . . and *three* to . . . *Wheeeee!*'

Minnie flings herself across the bed.

'That weren't 'alf smashing!' she puffs. 'I'm gonna 'ave another go.'

'Stoppit!' hisses Florrie, desperately. 'You've gone and woke up little Topsy. I can 'ear 'er crying.'

'Oh, just *one* more, Florrie.'

'No.'

Minnie is, as a rule, a wilful child, and she is wilful now.

'I'm gonna 'ave just one more go,' she says, staggering to keep her balance. '*One* to get ready – *two* to get steady – and *three* to – *Oooooow!*'

And Minnie tumbles off the bed with a thump that shakes the walls. On either side of Number 40 Myrdle Street, the neighbours hear her screams.

'Blessed kids!' cries Mrs Buckle. 'Why do we 'ave to 'ave 'em?'

Mr Buckle, who is shamming sleep beside his wife, does not answer her. With little Topsy wailing in her cot and Minnie bawling fit to raise the dead, it is – he gloomily reflects – it is without a doubt going to be another of those days.

Already, Mrs Buckle has hurried across the landing. Florrie is still sitting up in bed, clutching the counterpane beneath her chin, her eyes goggling with dismay.

'I told 'er, Mum. I told 'er not to do it.'

'Oh, my gawd!' says Mrs Buckle. 'What's she been and gorn and done?'

'She was doing diving – standing on the bed and doing diving. I told 'er not to. Honest, Mum, I did!'

'Diving! I'll give 'er diving!' Mrs Buckle grimly promises. 'Young madam!'

Seizing Minnie, she dumps her on the bed and works her arms and legs like pump handles, testing them for broken bones.

Charlie, meanwhile, watches hopefully from the door. If Minnie has not hurt herself, she may well get a smacking. But no smacks bruise her tender parts. Observing only that, if Minnie had been 'er *first*, there wouldn't have been a *second*, Mrs Buckle orders them all to get their clothes on and wash their hands and faces, and to be finished at the kitchen sink before she wants it, or there won't be no breakfast, no Southend, nor no nothing! – which last is very likely if their father is a-going to lay there snoring 'is 'ead off half the morning!

Her threats send Charlie scuttling off to skin the nightshirt over his head, search beneath the bed for socks and pants, struggle into his grey jersey, pull up his braces, and fasten his boots – polished especially the night before – with double knots. And so, first of all the family, he goes clumping down the stairs.

He edges past Albert's bike standing in the narrow passage, and goes into the kitchen, a gloomy room, its window darkened by the high brick wall between their house and Number 42. A sulphurous smell hangs in the air, and Charlie knows the gas-light's tiny pilot flame must have been blown out again. He clambers on a chair to reach the top bolt of the backyard door and steps into the brand new day. It strikes fresh upon his face.

Charlie enjoys the quiet of an early visit out the back, and sits listening to the dripping in the tank above his head and the crowing of a rooster in a neighbour's yard. When his eyes become accustomed to the half-light of the lav, he reaches for a piece of newspaper from the pile already neatly torn to size. The sheet he holds is part of the photograph of some battleships, and he begins to spell out the disjointed sentences that tell the story.

... and Dreadnoughts of the 3rd Battle Squadron were ...

... prove more than a match for German naval might shou ...

Uncle Jack's ship is one just like those with the funnels and great guns. Charlie wishes he were old enough to be a sailor and wear a uniform; then, if the war everyone keeps on about did start, he could help Uncle Jack to fire his gun and sink the Germans. Still, it is a pity Uncle has had to go back suddenly to Portsmouth. He was going to go to Southend with them and take them on a boat. You can catch some really big fish from a boat, out there in deep water.

The latch rattles as someone tries the door and startles Charlie.

'You in there?' calls Florrie.

'No!'

'What you doing then?'

'What d'you think?'

'Well, 'urry up . . . There's others wants to use it.'

Usually, Charlie would let Florrie do a dance. But today is different. In another minute, he has yanked the chain and fled before the water can gush into the pan.

On the kitchen window-sill a jam jar stands, half full of worms which Charlie unearthed yesterday after scratching and poking with a garden fork. He selects one now and watches it wriggle between his thumb and finger. It should do fine. As tempting a bit of bait, he thinks, as any fish could hope for. He pops it back and goes indoors to wash.

Minnie is already tip-toe at the sink, sulkily dabbling her fingers beneath the tap and sniffing now and then to remind the world that she has been ill-used. Charlie elbows in beside her, demanding his turn with the flannel. Then Florrie joins them and the three are bickering noisily when Mrs Buckle sweeps into the kitchen with little Topsy clamped beneath one arm.

'Florrie, 'ere, take baby for me . . . And just you get that clean frock wet, d'you hear, Minnie, and we'll leave you in the coal 'ole with the beetles! . . . *Albert!*' she shouts up the stairs. 'Albert! Just you come on down! Time you take over yourself these days we'll be gone afore you're ready.' She calls again. '*Dad!* . . . If

you want a shave before we goes, you'd better get up and have it. 'Course, if you'd rather go out looking like gawd knows what, well, I suppose that's your business!'

But upstairs Mr Buckle obediently heaves himself from the pillows and swings his feet down onto the floor.

In the tiny kitchen, the family breathe in and jostle past each other. Florrie tugs a comb through Minnie's sandy curls, does the fiddling hooks-and-eyes that fasten up her dress, straightens the bows of her clean pinafore, and catches Topsy, who is just about to overbalance from the chair where she's been planted out of danger's way. Charlie wolfs the rounds of bread and marge that Mrs Buckle cuts for breakfast.

Now, above the wailing of the baby, above Minnie's squeals and Mr Buckle's heavy footsteps on the stairs, the clatter of the milkman's cans and his '*Mee-yul-koo!*' reach Mrs Buckle's ears.

''Ere,' she says, and thrusts a jug into Charlie's hand. 'Go and get me 'alf a pint or none of you won't get a cup of tea. Yesterday's milk is only fit for making cheese. It just won't keep in this 'ot weather ... Gulp your food like that and you'll get the bellyache. It'll still be on your plate when you get back ... 'Ere's a penny, and make sure you get a proper canful. Do you hear?'

Little traffic finds its ways to Myrdle Street, only the regular procession of tradesmen's carts and barrows – the knife-grinder and the cat's-meat man, the coalman and the watercart, and, in summer time, an Italian ice cream seller. But every day sees the milkmen on their rounds.

Wally manages his three-wheeled cart with careless ease. The shining urn stands behind its rails, and into it Wally plunges his pint and half-pint measures.

'And what's yours?' he calls on seeing Charlie jug in hand. 'A pint of mild-and-bitter?'

'Just 'alf of milk,' Charlie answers back. 'And not too much water with it.'

'Nark it! Nark it!' Wally says. 'Talk like that could put me out of business. *Water!*' he exclaims, then quickly drops his voice. 'Water! Them cows is so stiff with cream, they 'as to be milked with spanners!'

Back in the kitchen, Mr Buckle finishes stropping his razor on the strap which hangs behind the door and begins to work up a lather with the brush.

''Course,' he says, 'there couldn't be no war, if your ordinary working man refused to fight. Where's the sense in working people a-killing of each other? 'Cos, let's face it, it ain't their war. They're not going to get nothing out of it either way. It's like I tried to explain to Jack.'

'He's only doing his job, ain't he?' replies Mrs Buckle. 'He's only doing as he's told.'

'That's my point!' protests Mr Buckle. 'That's just my point. It's high time working people stopped taking orders from them as has got the money.'

'Then who'd pay them?' asks Mrs Buckle obstinately.

'It's a matter of principle. It's a matter of what's right and what's wrong.'

'I'm sure our Jack wouldn't do nothing what's not right. Any'ow, he only does what he's told to do. When you're in the Navy, you takes orders.'

'But that's my point! I've just done telling yer. Working men have got to think for theirselves. They've got to decide for theirselves what's going to do them a bit of good. Let the Kaiser and the King blow each other's brains out of they wants to – and good riddance to them!'

'If I can't be a sailor like Uncle Jack,' says Charlie, who has come back with the milk, 'I think I'll be a soldier.'

Dad going on about his politics gets boring, but Charlie knows just what to say to make him mad.

'No son of mine . . . ' he starts to say. But, from the sandwiches she is cutting, Mrs Buckle glances at the clock that stands among a clutter of nick-nacks and ornaments on the mantelpiece.

'Look at the time!' she cries. 'If we're going to catch that train, we'll have to get our skates on. For gawd's sake, Bert, stop going on about yer war and make yourself look decent. Ada'll be 'ere hammering at the door afore we knows it.'

'And who needs more battleships when they've got Ada Hackett?' her brother-in-law mutters into his shaving-mug.

Ada Hackett has remained a single lady, which is – as Mr Buckle sees it – a blessing for any man who might have changed her situation. As a young woman she went into service and rose to the heights of lady's maid. But, some years ago, Aunt Ada returned home to live with their widowed mother in the little house just round the corner in Settles Street. There, by taking in 'Superior Needlework – Ladies' Lingerie and Wedding Trousseaux a Speciality' and with the five shillings weekly pension that old Mrs Hackett is entitled to, she just manages to keep them both, if not in comfort, at least outside the workhouse.

Just now, a knock announces her arrival.

'There's your auntie,' Mrs Buckle says. 'Florrie, go and let her in . . . Bert! For gawd's sake, get a move on! You're still in your shirtsleeves, and you know how particular Ada is about that sort of thing.'

'Perhaps,' says Mr Buckle, 'if she hadn't been so particular, she might have had the chance of seeing a man without no shirt at all.'

'*Bert!*' Mrs Buckle pleads.

Already it's too late. With Florrie trotting meekly after her, Aunt Ada has processed into the kitchen, robed for the occasion in her best dress, the black sateen, and her jets.

''Ello, Ada,' says Mrs Buckle. 'We're all a bit be'ind.'

'Like the 'orse's tail,' puts in Mr Buckle.

'Still, it looks like being a nice day,' Mrs Buckle hurries on.

'Well, you can't never rightly tell with weather,' observes Aunt Ada. 'We had rain yesterday, so I don't see why we shouldn't have some more today. Not that I feel much like a holiday. And I don't really know as I ought to leave Mother, not with Jack going off sudden like he did. She's taken it bad, you know.'

'Yes.' Mrs Buckle sighs and tuts as she agrees. 'Yes, if it was just me, I wouldn't leave the 'ouse. They was saying the other day in Lewinses that the first thing we'll know about it, if they really starts a war, is the Kaiser sending them airships over and dropping things down on our 'eads. It don't seem possible, do it? ... But there's the kids. We'd promised the kids. Not that *some* of them deserves it!'

Minnie pouts and sticks a licked finger in the sugar basin.

'I suppose you heard,' confides Aunt Ada, 'what they did to Schmitts last night?'

'The bakers down off Cable Street?' says Mrs Buckle. 'No.'

'Smashed the windows!'

'They never did!'

'Blimey!' breaks in Mr Buckle. 'Where's the sense in that? Schmitts has been there for donkey's years. Now they're supposed to be German spies, is that it?'

'I'm sure I don't know about that,' Aunt Ada says. 'But you can't change what you're born. A lot of trouble would be saved if people stayed in their own countries. That's all I say.'

'But those Schmitts was *born* here!' argues Mr Buckle. 'In any case ....'

'A cup of tea, Ada?' Mrs Buckle interrupts him. 'There should be another in the pot. If there ain't none left for young Albert, that's his own lookout.'

'Why?' Aunt Ada asks. 'What's he doing?'

'Gawd knows! It's all along of this 'ere girl, if you asks me.'

'Girl?'

'Yerse. Met her at work, 'e did.'

'What, at the fish shop?'

'No. She 'elps out in that little draper's just opposite. Know where I mean?'

'Oh, Chataways. Used to have a boy there with one eye?'

'That's the place. Well, he's met this girl – Letty – and you've never seen the likes of it ... Moody! You can't say nothing to him. And spends 'alf his time combing his hair and sniffing at his fingers to see if they smells of fish.'

'But he's only – what is it – sixteen!' exclaims Aunt Ada. 'Whatever are you thinking of to allow it, Ruby?'

'It's nature, ain't it?' says Mr Buckle, drying his face. 'It's natural at his age to start sitting up and taking notice.'

'And we all know what "natural" leads to,' says Aunt Ada. 'And if *you* don't, who does?'

In the awkward silence that follows this remark, Albert comes into the kitchen and is quick to notice the thoughtful stares directed at him.

'Well, what's the matter?' he demands.

'Never you mind,' replies his mother.

'Aren't you going to say hello to your auntie?' Aunt Ada asks.

''Ello,' says Albert, and pushes through the family to wash himself.

'And is you-know-who coming with us?' Aunt Ada whispers in her funeral and operations voice.

'No, she ain't!' calls Albert from the sink. 'And for

two pins I wouldn't neither!'

'Now then,' warns Mr Buckle. 'Manners!'

'Well . . . ' grumbles Albert as he scrubs his hands.

'*Well!*' declares Aunt Ada. 'Whatever next!'

Charlie, by now, has gobbled down his breakfast and slips outside to see if anything is happening in the street.

In one of the whiskery loops of rope that dangle from a lamp-post, Charlie's friend and class-mate, Sidney Springett, sits idly swinging. Sidney is wearing his boots in honour of the holiday, and Charlie knows the hiding he will get if his mother catches him kicking the toes against the cast-iron standard and the kerb.

'Wotcher, Sid!' he calls.

'Wotcher, Charlie!' Sid replies, and comes scuffing to a halt. 'Still reckon you're going to catch something?'

''Course!'

Sidney laughs. 'A cold, p'raps, when you falls in.'

'Oh, yeah!' says Charlie. 'Well, you just wait 'till I get back and shows yer – big ones!'

'You won't catch nothing.'

'Wanna bet?'

'What with?' says Sidney. 'Ain't got a button to me name – except me flies. I've had to pinch some of Mabel's hairpins to keep me decent.' And he twangs his braces to show the pins bent double that hitch them to his trousers.

'I got a railey,' Charlie boasts. 'Won it off of Bigsie Fletcher.' He thrusts a hand into his pocket and pulls out a bright brass button that lies gleaming in his palm.

'It's a prime'n. Listen!' He throws the button to the pavement where it rings to prove its worth. Sidney slips nimbly from his rope and stoops to pick it up.

'Gi's it!' Charlie snaps. ''Smine!'

'All right, all right! 'Ere y'are. I'm only looking, ain't I!'

Charlie restores the button to the safety of his pocket, and turns it over and over, fingering the embossed coat of arms.

'Toss yer for it,' Sidney offers.

'Come off it!' Charlie says. 'You ain't got nothing to bet with.'

'Couple of bonks,' Sidney says, holding out two marbles. 'I'd forgotten these.'

Charlie does not give them half a glance. 'Nar! Ain't worth nothing like my railey.'

'Ah, go on,' Sidney pleads.

'Nar,' says Charlie. 'Nuffin doing.'

'You shonk!' Sidney mutters.

'What d'yer call me?'

'Nuffin, nuffin.'

'I ain't no shonk, and I'll knock yer face off if you says I am!'

'All right, all right – you ain't then.'

Sidney resumes his aimless swinging round the lamp-post.

'Well, when you all a-going?' he asks.

'Soon,' says Charlie. 'We got to be at Fenchurch Street by nine o'clock. What you doing today?'

'Nuffin. With Dad on strike, we can't go nowhere.'

'My dad says your dad's lot is bound to win. London

can't manage long without its builders, 'e says.'

Sidney nods, but thinks of the weeks and weeks of skimpy meals, his mother's nagging about no money, and the rows which ended with his father slamming out of doors.

'Your Uncle Jack still going with you?'

'Oh, 'e got this telegram on Sunday. He had to be back on his ship last night, ready for the war.'

'It's all they talks about,' Sidney complains. 'Their bloomin' war ... and strikes!'

'It's a pity about Uncle Jack,' Charlie carries on, ''cos he was going to take us on a boat. Still, 'e give me a tanner to spend. Dad's looking after it for me. It's a new one. All shiny. This year's ... 1914. You should see it! I'm gonna buy ice cream and bull's-eyes, and have a go on one of them telescopes on the pier, and ....'

Without any warning, Sidney swings at Charlie, kicking him in the stomach, and sends him sprawling.

''Ope you lose yer blasted tanner!' Sidney shouts, cuffing aside his tears, and races off down the street.

Charlie struggles, panting to his feet, just as Florrie calls to him from the door.

'Charlie! Mum says you're to come this minute. It's almost time to go.'

He dares not disobey. Screaming his promise of revenge, he follows Florrie back into the house.

The kitchen is now a fumbling of coat buttons and a straightening of hats, as the Buckles and Aunt Ada make final adjustments to themselves in readiness for the 'off'.

'And, if you wants that spade and bucket, then you carries them,' Mrs Buckle is informing Minnie. 'Your aunt and me 'as got our 'ands full, what with the baskets and the baby... Charlie, pull your cap the right way round. Looks like you've been heaving coal.'

'Me rod! I 'aven't got me rod!' cries Charlie, rushing up the stairs.

'Why couldn't you have it ready, instead of playing in the streets?' Mrs Buckle calls out after him. 'Right now, Ada, if you can take that basket, and Albert takes the other one, and Florrie carries that bag with the fruit. Your dad can bring that one with the towels and things, while I look after Topsy. Now, is that everything?'

'Well, we ain't got the kitchen sink,' Mr Buckle grumbles.

'Ooh, the cat, Mum!' squeals Florrie. 'She's still in 'ere!'

'Blessed thing!' says Mrs Buckle. 'Quick, put 'er out the back.'

'But she ain't finished breakfast yet,' says Minnie.

'Shall I put her saucer outside with her?' Florrie asks.

'What! And have all the cats in creation round here!' exclaims Mrs Buckle. 'I should think so!'

And Primrose finds herself plucked from her morning dish of bits and dumped in the backyard with the door bolted in her face.

Outside, the party assembles on the pavement, as Mr Buckle locks the front door and drops the key into his pocket. Now, they set off, Mrs Buckle with little Topsy and Aunt Ada at the front, Mr Buckle behind them, followed by Albert trying to catch a glance of himself reflected in the front room window; then come Florrie and Minnie, with Charlie bringing up the rear, proudly carrying his rod like a little standard bearer.

They have reached the corner of Myrdle Street when Charlie stops and cries, 'Me worms! I've forgot me worms!'

'You should 'ave thought of them before,' says Mrs Buckle. 'As it is, we'll be lucky if we don't miss that train.'

Charlie begins to whimper.

'But, Mum, I need them.'

'Look,' says Mr Buckle, 'I'll run back with him and we'll catch you up. We'll only be a jiffy. Come on, Charlie. It ain't nothing to cry about.'

Without waiting for any argument, he turns Charlie round and they hurry home. The backdoor is unbolted; Charlie runs to fetch his jar; and Primrose slips back in.

'Now then,' says Mr Buckle, when he and Charlie are in the street again, 'best foot forward or we'll neither of us hear the end of it!'

Chapter 2

The Buckles are not the only Londoners to make an early start on this August Bank Holiday. Like them, other families already make their way to Fenchurch Street to catch the Southend trains. And horse brakes and wagonettes, their passengers in high feather and hallooing to pedestrians, rattle, clop and jingle past them bound for the fair on Chingford Plains or picnics and rambles in Epping Forest. And no vehicle is in better spirits than a little coster's cart, a donkey between the shafts, and the entire family – bowler-hatted father with the reins, mother nursing baby, daughters squeezed in behind, sons perched legs a-dangle at the back – all accommodated somehow in or

on it, and all confident that it is going to be a splendid day.

Mrs Buckle marches her party down Commercial Road – Minnie has been told twice already not to dawdle – through side turnings, across Mansell Street and along the narrow roads in the shadow of the viaduct which bring them to the station. And, when they turn the corner, they find the forecourt is already thronged with trippers; fathers counting heads, missing little Willy or counting him twice over; mothers fussing with baskets, bags and parcels; children whining, grizzling, wandering off and getting lost. The sherbet-and-water man finds he does brisk business and the pennies rattle into the pudding basin which serves him for a cash-box. And, as a prelude to the seaside entertainment, three black-faced minstrels are playing on the concertina, the banjo and penny whistle, and dancing too.

Charlie loves it all, the crowds, the bustle, the sense of something just about to happen.

''Ere, Dad,' he says, 'do you think . . . ?'

'Not now, Charlie,' Mr Buckle says, reaching in his pocket.

Above the hubbub there rises the sing-song clamour of a news-vendor.

'Spe-shal! . . . Invasion of France . . . Germany's Ul-timatum to Belgium . . . England and the war . . . Paper!'

Customers besiege him and he cannot pull the papers from the bundles on his arm or take the money fast enough. In a couple of minutes all his stock is gone.

'There's no stopping it now,' says Mr Buckle, shaking his head over the copy he has bought.

'Dad . . . ' Charlie tries again.

But Mr Buckle can't be bothered with him.

'Quiet,' he says. 'Can't yer see I'm reading?'

'Never mind about yer paper!' Mrs Buckle says. 'Do something useful and go and get the tickets. You're worse than a kid with his nose stuck in a comic.'

'All right! All right!' says Mr Buckle. 'You coming with me, Albert? The rest of yer stay 'ere. We shan't be long.'

'Better not be!' Mrs Buckle warns. 'Not unless you want to 'ave a picnic on the pavement 'ere.'

'Plenty of time! There's plenty of time!' Mr Buckle taps his pocket watch. 'There's another fourteen minutes before the off.'

'Bert Buckle, if we're too late to find a seat, I don't go, and that's telling yer!'

'All right! All right! Blimey! Come on, Albert.'

'Well,' grumbles Mrs Buckle to her sister, 'it's always the same. Leaves things to the last minute. Always does. And you know what it was like last year. So crowded there was even kids up in the luggage racks.'

'That's *men* for you!' Aunt Ada sniffs. And, saying that, makes it plain that she has said all that need be said of so disagreeable a subject.

Charlie fidgets, impatient to get started, while they wait for Mr Buckle to return. He wonders grown-ups don't think going to the seaside more important and exciting than their newspapers and wars.

'Mum, can I sit by the winder?' Minnie asks, hoping to get her bid in first.

'You'll sit just where you're told – that is, if you get a seat at all. You've been nothing but a nuisance since the moment you woke up. And it's no good you pulling faces!'

Mr Buckle comes back at last, with Albert trailing gloomily behind him.

'Now,' he says, 'Charlie, Minnie, listen will yer. *Listen* I said! When they open the gates, you two go straight through with the crowds. Don't 'ang around for us, d'you hear? And, if anyone asks you who you're with, say Mum and Dad have gone on through already and you've got left behind them in the rush, see?'

They see; they've done this before, but it's not something you get used to. However, if it means going to Southend or not going to Southend, there's no point arguing.

At a word from Mr Buckle, his party gather up their traps, advance beneath the fretted canopy, through the station doors, leaving the sunshine for the gloom inside, and begin to climb the broad flights of stairs that lead up to the platforms.

The great, glass-vaulted roof echoes to the gunfire of carriage doors, the hiss of steam, deafening bursts of chuffing from impatient engines. Where the barrier is beset with trippers a blackboard announces in chalked capitals: SOUTHEND EXCURSION.

'Right, Charlie,' Mr Buckle warns, 'hold tight to Minnie's hand . . . 'Course we won't lose you, you silly girl! Just keep a-hold of Charlie and you'll be quite all right. And don't go looking round for us. *We*'ll come and get *you*.'

As he speaks the gates are opened.

'Well, go on,' Mr Buckle growls, prodding Charlie forward. 'Don't 'ang about!'

'I don't wanna go!' Minnie grizzles, as Charlie drags her after him.

The crowds close in behind them and they are trapped in the shuffling movement towards the narrow gap through which they have to pass. An elbow knocks Charlie's cap sideways; the corner of a basket strikes him in the mouth; and bodies in smothering serge and bombazine hem him in. Minnie clings to Charlie, and Charlie holds on to her and struggles with his other hand to keep his rod from poking someone in the eye.

Collectors calling out for tickets to be ready warn him that the really dangerous moment has arrived. Now, experience on previous occasions has taught Charlie to attach himself to some other family and hope an extra one or two will not be noticed by the harassed railway staff, and the party just in front sounds disorganised and numerous.

'Wally! Rosie! . . . Where's Rosie? Where's . . . Oh, so there you are? . . . Alfred stop doing that or you won't get no nice okey-pokey at the seaside.'

'Gawd! Where's the tickets got to? I 'ad 'em in me 'and . . . I know I 'ad 'em in me 'and.'

'No, Sidney. *You* wanted them, so just *you* carry 'em!'

'I know I 'ad 'em in me 'and!'

'Where's Rosie got to now? If you do that again,

Freddy, I'll give you such a smacking!'

'They were in me 'and!'

'Oh, come on, Frank! You're 'olding everybody up.'

'I tell you they were . . . .'

'So what d'you do with them when you picked the baskets up?'

'Well, I must 'ave put them in . . . .'

'. . . in your weskit pocket! Oh, there's times you've no more sense than these 'ere kids!'

'Now, come on, mate,' the collector pleads. 'The engine's running out of steam. All right, missus, take 'em through. The old man'll catch you up.'

The crowds behind press forward, and Charlie and Minnie scuttle through on the lee side of the mother who escorts her flotilla of unruly children to the platform.

They have made it.

Now, just go on a little further and wait for Mum and Dad. That's the plan. But Minnie stops and turns round to see her family at the very moment they are passing through the barrier. Relief and yearning overwhelm her.

'*Mum!*'

Above the racket preliminary to steam locomotion, Minnie's howls rise very loud and all too clear. Mrs Buckle looks; Mr Buckle looks; Aunt Ada looks; all the people on the platform stop and look; and the ticket collector, who has just punched five tickets and handed them back to Mr Buckle, looks up to see a little girl – pursued by a little boy – running with arms outstretched to the lady whom he has just admitted to

the platform.

Mrs Buckle afterwards declares (repeatedly) that she thinks she could have died of shame. As it is, she is even more inclined to make an end of Minnie.

The ticket collector may be too busy marshalling the holidaymakers through before the train pulls out, or he may be a family man himself and sympathises with the Buckles' economies; at any rate, he does not ask what Minnie and Charlie are doing on his platform, contenting himself with a stare at Mr Buckle which plainly says, 'Oh, yes, I know all about your little game.'

The glum, embarrassed party slinks along the train searching for a compartment to themselves. Things take a turn for the better when, about three-quarters of the way down, Mr Buckle spots one that is completely empty.

'Right, everybody in,' he orders. 'Mum and Topsy first. Florrie, Albert, pass the baskets up to your Auntie Ada . . . and you can stop that pushing, Charlie. Try and be a gentleman.'

The door slams to behind them, and they sink onto the seats, congratulating one another on their unexpected luck. All except Aunt Ada, who glances suspiciously about her.

'Why's this one been left empty I should like to know?'

Her dark words stir a moment of disquiet, and in anxious silence they all look about them at the floor, the roof, the upholstery, and sniff the air.

'There ain't nothing wrong with this,' is Mr Buckle's judgement. 'Just ain't so many people about, that's all.'

'That's true,' Mrs Buckle says. 'It ain't like last year. Talk about crowds! I ain't never seen nothing like it. I suppose it's the building strike. People just haven't got the money now for outings.'

'People who won't do no work,' Aunt Ada snorts, 'can't expect to have money for no joy-rides. And I don't know what the world's coming to when they do!'

'Blimey!' retorts Mr Buckle. 'So a man can sweat his guts out for a pittance and that's all right, is it?'

'If he didn't think the wages good enough, he shouldn't 'ave took the job on.'

'But there ain't no other jobs.'

'So beggars can't be choosers.'

'It's bad enough when you hear the bosses talk like that,' Mr Buckle cries, 'but when it's one of your own class ... !'

'It's a good job some of us are still in our right senses!'

'Oh, stop it, do!' Mrs Buckle says. 'Argufying won't change nothing. And this is supposed to be a 'oliday, not one of your political meetings in Victoria Park.'

Mr Buckle raises his finger to continue the debate, but he is prevented by the unexpected opening of the carriage door and a hearty bellow.

'Come on, girl! There's room in 'ere!'

All the Buckles turn in deep dismay to see who these intruders are. The stout figure of a woman enters first, supported from behind. Then a man of like build struggles in and collapses by his wife. Last, a girl of Florrie's age steps lightly from the platform and sits down opposite her parents.

There is a final salvo of closing doors; the guard blows his whistle; and the train gives a violent jolt.

'What-ho, she bumps!' the fat man roars, grinning round the company. 'I do believe as 'ow we're off!'

Chapter 3

The Buckles study the newcomers in uneasy silence; but they, nothing abashed, return their stares with the utmost affability and unconcern.

Father is clad in a suit of green and orange checks, and a gold watch chain with heavy links hangs across his stomach. At length, he puffs, removes his derby, and mops his glistening pate with a green silk handkerchief; then runs it round the greasy leather band before restoring the hat at a jaunty angle to his head.

'Strewth!' he declares. 'It's going to be an 'ot 'un.'

His wife, resplendent in mauve satin and fox fur stole, beams her approval of the observation and fans

herself with the lacy handkerchief she clutches.

'Told 'er not to wear them furs,' the fat man chortles. 'On a day like this them animals is thanking their lucky stars as they can go running round in the *rude* – beg your pudden – *nude*! Ha, ha, ha, ha, ha!'

This little sally earns a peal of laughter from the lady and a playful dig in the waistcoat with her elbow. The effect it produces on the Buckles is not so gratifying. None of them finds very much to like about these swanky people; and Mr Buckle wonders how any honest working man can be so well-to-do in these hard times.

Florrie, out of the corner of her eye, looks enviously at the daughter. Poor Florrie, plain as suet pudding, how she admires the mass of silky curls beneath the smart straw hat, the neat nose and mouth, hands in spotless cotton gloves folded on the lap! Then the girl turns her head and stares at Florrie. Her cool, grey eyes examine Florrie without haste. She smiles faintly to herself, before she gives her attention to the view of Stepney's roofs and chimney pots as the train runs along the viaduct.

From beneath lowered brows, Albert compares her with his Letty. He faces up to facts; sniffs his fingers while making out to scratch his nose and wonders if he'll get a chance to speak to her.

His philandering designs are interrupted by the hiss and snarl of quarrelling.

''Tis!'

''Tisn't!'

''Tis!'

"'Tisn't! 'Tisn't!"

"'Tis!"

'Oh, what is it this time?' groans Mrs Buckle. 'Ain't there never no peace when you two gets together?'

'It's *'er*!' says Charlie. 'I keep on telling 'er that castle place afore you gets to Southend's on the other side. But she won't 'ave it. I told 'er we picked these seats so's we could see the sea – So there! – I'm right, ain't I, Dad?'

"'Ang on,' says Mr Buckle. 'I've lost me bearings. Now, if we're going this way....'

'Not much doubt about that!' the fat man chuckles.

'If we're going this way,' repeats Mr Buckle, 'if we're going this way, and if I was facing the way we was going, then the river would be on my left – No, wait a minute – is it me right? Yerse, it must be me right – I think.'

'Well, is the sea on our side or ain't it?' demands Charlie.

'It's not, young man,' Aunt Ada tells him. 'And, if you was mine, you wouldn't speak twice to me like that.'

'Your auntie's right,' says Mrs Buckle. 'Mind yer manners!'

Any disappointment Minnie feels at finding herself on the wrong side of the carriage is more than offset by the satisfaction of seeing Charlie on the wrong side of everybody else.

Charlie struggles to choke back the tears. His heart has been set on that first glimpse of a muddy creek and boats tied to their moorings, sights which seem to call:

'The sea! The sea! Not far to the sea!' And now these awful people have come and got the seaside windows. Try as he will, a tear slips over his eyelid and trickles down his cheek.

'Nah then, nah then, John-Willy,' the fat man jollies him. 'Keep your pecker up, as the 'en said to the poor old cock.'

His wife is moved to speech.

'Ah, never mind then, cherub. When we get near the seaside, you and the little girl can come and sit on my lap.'

'And why just them two, may I ask?' enquires the fat man, winking round the carriage. 'There's room enough on there for all the family!'

'Oh, stop it, Archy, for goodness' sake!' the lady squeals. 'I don't know what the gentleman and these ladies 'ere will think of us, I'm sure.'

'Now, that's ever so kind of you,' says Mrs Buckle, 'but you don't want kids climbing over that nice new dress. And, in any case, they don't deserve it, carrying on like that.'

'Ah, let them,' the fat lady beams. 'They're only kids.'

'No, really. They're making a lot of fuss about nothing. You'd think when we got to Southend we wasn't going to let them off the train, the way they're carrying on.'

The fat lady is reluctant to give in. 'Oh – look at their little faces!'

The expression on those faces is that of horror at the prospect of being made to sit upon the lap.

'I don't hold with being soft on children what get the sulks,' says Aunt Ada loftily.

Mr Buckle finds the conversation wearing. 'How about a bite of something?' he says. 'I think I could manage a bit of this and that, and it's a goodish way to go. Come on, what you got for us, Ruby?'

In spite of Mrs Buckle's complaints about people who must have hollow legs, and its not being an hour since they had their breakfasts, baskets of provisions are taken down and sandwiches and apples handed round. When the family has been supplied, Mrs Buckle holds out an opened parcel to the couple opposite.

'Go on, help yourselves,' she says. 'We've plenty 'ere, and you don't look as though you've got none.'

The fat man declines her offer with a flapping of one hand.

'No thanks, love – not for me and the missus. We'll have a spot of lunch at an hotel. It's our outing really. We're not ones for the beach. No, a nice spot of lunch with a bottle of something good. Then perhaps a stroll to let it all slip down; a nice shellfish tea – 'cos, let's face it, you can't go to Southend and not 'ave a cockle or a whelk or two.'

''Ark at 'im!' his wife chimes in. 'A cockle or a whelk or two, he says!' She pokes him in the stomach. ''E never got all that on just a cockle or a whelk or two!'

Bravely, Mrs Buckle still offers up her humble fare. 'Oh, won't you have just one?'

The fat man leans forward and turns back the corner of a sandwich.

'Fish-paste ... no thanks, really, love. Fish-paste 'angs around so; won't let you forget it. We always likes to start our lunch off with a morsel of smoked salmon, and after fish-paste you just wouldn't get the flavour.'

Mr Buckle likes the fat man less and less.

'Smoked salmon?' he says. 'Must be something like kippers, I suppose.'

'Well, 'ardly, 'ardly,' demurs the fat man with a smile. 'Not at the price it is. Oh, it's shocking expensive - shocking!'

'Shocking!' echoes his lady. 'It's 'ardly right to buy it. But, then, if it's there, someone's got to eat it or it'll just go to waste. So my Archy always pays up no matter what it is.'

'Perhaps your little girl ... ?' murmurs Mrs Buckle, reaching the parcel across Mr Buckle to where the girl sits in silence, staring through the window.

'Spots!' her mother says. 'Paste always brings her out in spots.'

Florrie, reminded of a fiery pimple on her neck, ponders for the first time the advisability of consuming fish-paste sandwiches, but deciding that any damage has been done, munches on.

The train has left the brick and roof-slate acres of the London suburbs and clatters through the open country. The sun shines brightly. On the embankment, smoke shadows scurry by. And, beside the track, cores and orange peel and screwed-up paper bags mark the route the excursionists have taken. Charlie and Minnie are kept amused by counting cows and horses that flash past in their dreamy meadows, and waving to distant figures which stop and stand to watch them hurry on their journey to the sea.

Offended by the fish-paste episode, Mr Buckle has pulled out his copy of *The Herald*, but he has not been reading many minutes when he folds the paper to single out an article and stab at it with a law-down-laying finger.

'Now *that's* telling you!'

'Telling us what?' replies the fat man.

'That there ain't no member – no *thinking* member – of the working classes what reckons we've got any call to go and get ourselves mixed up with this war that's brewing on the Continent.'

'Oh – and who the hell says that then?'

'Look, this demonstration yesterday in Trafalgar Square. They were all up there on the platform – your Independent Labour Party, the Union Boys, Keir Hardie, George Lansbury. And they all said the same thing: "Keep Britain out of the war!" I was there meself. I heard them.'

'And they calls theirselves Englishmen!' exclaims the fat man. 'Then they ought to be ashamed of theirselves, they did! And that's a fact!'

'Look, mate,' says Mr Buckle, 'with thirty thousand workers locked out by the bosses, this ain't no time for playing soldiers out in Belgium.'

The fat man smoulders a deeper red.

'Where's yer pride in yer country? Where's yer sense of British honour?'

'Don't talk to me about British honour, mate,' says Mr Buckle. 'I'll tell you about British honour. British honour's locking a bloke out of his job for twenty-five weeks for being in a union – twenty-five weeks! He's got a wife and kids, ain't 'e, and damn-all to keep them on. So in the end he 'angs hisself . . . It happened to a carpenter down our way last week. That's your British honour. Ask 'er if you don't believe me. That's right, ain't it, Ruby?'

Mrs Buckle looks distressed, and holds little Topsy closer to her.

'Don't go on about it, Albert. It don't do any good.'

''Course it don't do any good,' agrees the fat man. 'People generally gets what they deserve.'

Mr Buckle struggles to control himself.

'Look, mate, there's this old girl I knows of lives in Hackney. Her 'usband was killed on the railways. She ain't old enough for a pension. Got no family to help her out, so she's in the workhouse, see. Well, one of the Board of Guardians has the nerve to tell his chums that he thinks it's a bit 'ard that the poor only get dry bread to eat, and he suggests the Parish might run to a drop of syrup or a scrape of dripping to help it down. My gawd! You'd have thought he was asking for the earth. "A sensational statement." That's what they said asking for a bit of bread and dripping was! So that poor old girl's still managing on a couple of slices of dry bread a day and you sit there and tell me she gets what she deserves! Well, you tell me what *you've* done to deserve smoked salmon what's so shocking expensive!'

'Now then, there ain't no need for getting personal,' the fat man angrily retorts. 'I don't have to sit here and be insulted by the likes of you!'

'So what you going to do about it? Stop the train and tell the guard to have us ordered off? We've as much right here as you!'

In his rage, Mr Buckle is heedless of the two little Buckles who are travelling without a ticket. But the other Buckles are not. Dad has gone too far. Mrs Buckle grips his arm.

Mr Buckle, feeling the pressure of her fingers, understands. Not that there is really any danger, he decides. The train isn't going to stop until they reach Southend, and it isn't likely that that there greedy-guts will pull the communication cord because he'd been rude about his rotten old smoked salmon.

'Any Englishman ought to be proud to wear his country's uniform,' the fat man grumbles, ostensibly for the information of his wife.

'Then you'll be volunteering, I suppose,' says Mr Buckle.

The fat man turns a scornful eye on Mr Buckle. 'If my doctor would allow me, which he wouldn't. And, besides, I've got a business what demands my attendance daily.'

'Oh, yerse,' says Mr Buckle. 'And what's this business of such national importance that stops you changing your doctor for a more patriotic one?'

'Now, don't you come the high and mighty with me. I could buy the likes of you up ten times over and not bother with the change.'

'Yerse, but I'm not up for sale!'

'Not yet, you ain't,' the fat man answers. 'But I've had hundreds like you in the shop with their pocket watches and their teaspoons; then it's sheets and blankets and their bits of furniture – anything they can raise a bob on. Oh, very haughty they are when they first comes in; you'd think they was doing me a favour. But they change their tune!'

'My gawd!' says Mr Buckle. '*A pawnbroker!*'

Mr Buckle is a worker, a craftsman: he takes wood and turns it into tables, chairs and cupboards – things that people need. To him the pawnbroker's shop stands for all he hates in a world where money can make more money, but a life of useful labour be rewarded with the workhouse.

'My gawd!' says Mr Buckle. 'No wonder he can afford to stuff hisself with salmon. It's as good a business as an undertaker's – better, in fact, 'cos he don't even 'ave to wait until we're dead!'

There is no more to be said.

For long minutes, no one speaks; only Topsy coos and dribbles. Inside each head is the same longing to arrive at journey's end and escape. But, until then, they must sit together, knee to knee, with eyes averted.

It is Florrie's desperate whimper that restores some movement to their stiffening necks.

'Mum! *Mum!*'

'Well, what is it?'

'I feel sick!'

Florrie becomes, at once, the object of anxious contemplation. It is not a corridor train. The fat man and his wife exchange glances as if to say 'what else can you expect?'

'Oh, *Mum! Mum!*'

The sensation of being on the point of vomiting is terrible enough: to be trapped in a railway carriage, knowing the revulsion she inspires in her companions is almost worse.

'We can always rely on *you*, can't we!' says Mrs Buckle.

'It's all this getting over-excited,' declares Aunt Ada; which is a gross injustice, for, all the while, Florrie has sat there as demurely as a nun.

''Ere,' calls Mrs Buckle, taking command of a ticklish situation, 'Charlie, Minnie, quick! Mind yourselves!'

Charlie and Minnie press back into their seats as Mrs Buckle seizes Florrie by the shoulders and thrusts her head out of the open window.

The wind whips away her bonnet, roars in her ears and streams the sandy hair across her face, while, below, the sleepers and the trackside vegetation race backwards in a dizzy blur. In a spinning universe of lunatic disorder, Florrie, unheard, weeps and retches, until she is hauled back into the shelter of the carriage and propped up in her seat, sobbing, shivering and hatless. Then Mrs Buckle's arm is round her roughly comforting, and with a handkerchief she mops the damp and pallid face.

'Now then, love, you'll feel better now, you see. It's all up now ... Mind you, it's a pity about your hat.'

But, for the present, hats do not matter much to Florrie, who is only just beginning to feel any satisfaction in being still alive.

Mrs Buckle glances across the carriage and catches a

thoughtful and preoccupied expression in Charlie's eye.

'Oh, no you don't, young man. One of you is quite enough. Just you play I-Spy or something with Minnie and keep your mind off you-know-what.'

'I don't want to play no soppy games with 'er!' says Charlie. 'I ain't gonna be sick.' And he turns away and glares out of his window, just as their train roars through a station in a cloud of smoke and flying sparks. The name spins Charlie round. 'It's Pitsea! It's Pitsea! I saw it wrote up on a board. It ain't far now is it? Not when it says "*sea*".'

'It's quite a bit yet,' Mr Buckle cautions Charlie, adding that he doesn't rightly know how Pitsea came to get its name.

Again, Charlie looks enviously at the other end of the compartment. He longs to press his nose against the window, eager to catch the first glimpse of the sea. But, of course, the window seats are occupied. Why, thinks Charlie, why had those people picked on their compartment? Or why couldn't they have been another minute late? Then they would have missed the train. But there sit the fat man and his wife, and no amount of wishing can make them disappear. And that girl, their daughter, taking up a corner seat, half the time she isn't looking out at all, but smooths the fingers of her gloves and looks with faint amusement at poor Florrie.

Young Albert thinks about the fat man's daughter too. In fact, hasn't thought of much else since she appeared. Before Dad's bust-up with her father, he had decided she was quite a bit of all right and that what Letty didn't know wasn't going to grieve her. But, Dad, of course, had to wreck his chances with his politics and the War! He still keeps looking sideways at the girl. Now what is she smiling at? Is his hair sticking up again? Or is his collar crooked? Did she sniff just then? Oh, damn the fish shop! A girl like that was never going to fancy a bloke who smelt of 'addocks, eels and bloaters!

So they are all carried to Southend. Mr Buckle studies his newspaper. Mrs Buckle restrains little Topsy, who whines and wriggles on her lap. Aunt Ada stares stonily at a print of Felixstowe above the heads of the fat man and his wife, who sit, stiff and sulky, opposite. And Charlie all the time stands in a fever of expectation, gazing down the carriage seaward, while Minnie plays with the leather strap used to raise and lower the window.

Then, at Benfleet, the creek which runs like a railway siding from the estuary, winds into view. The tide is flowing, and dinghies bob and barges wallow in the rising water. Now only mast-heads are visible above the bright green tufted banks, until the train runs along the level plain created by the Dutchmen who drained the foreshore of the Thames a century ago. On the left, the ruins of Hadleigh Castle still sleep at their post as guardians of the river. Now Leigh-on-Sea and lines of cocklesheds. Only the seawall between the railway track and waves that dance and sparkle in the sunshine. Next, Chalkwell. Then just snooty Westcliff before they will steam, at last, into Southend Central.

Time to straighten hats and re-tie bedraggled bows;

time to reach down baskets, bundles, spades and buckets from the luggage rack; time to search through waistcoat pockets for the tickets.

The Buckles are up and busy with their preparations, when, with a screech of brakes and a crash of buffers, the train lurches and jolts to a halt. Mrs Buckle clutches Topsy safely to her, but Charlie and Minnie are thrown down to the floor, while Mr Buckle sits heavily on Albert. The fat man is flung into Aunt Ada's lap, and his wife's eyes pop from under the feathers of her hat which has been pushed forward at a drunken angle. Opposite, her daughter wails and tries to staunch a bleeding nose, the victim of her mother's parasol.

When the train is still, cries of alarm give place to angry demands to know what the 'ell is going on.

'Oh, my gawd!' moans Mrs Buckle. "As it started? Is it the Germans, Albert?'

'Don't be stupid, woman!' her husband reassures her. He then props Florrie up against the seat back and sticks his head out of the window to see what is going on.

From every carriage heads are poking, twisting left and right in search of information.

'What's up, mate?' enquires Mr Buckle of an adjacent head.

'Dunno. Thought we was coming off the rails or something. But I can't see nothing wrong.'

'D'you think some barmy geezer could have gone and pulled the communication cord?'

'I'll give him something to pull it for! It was lucky I

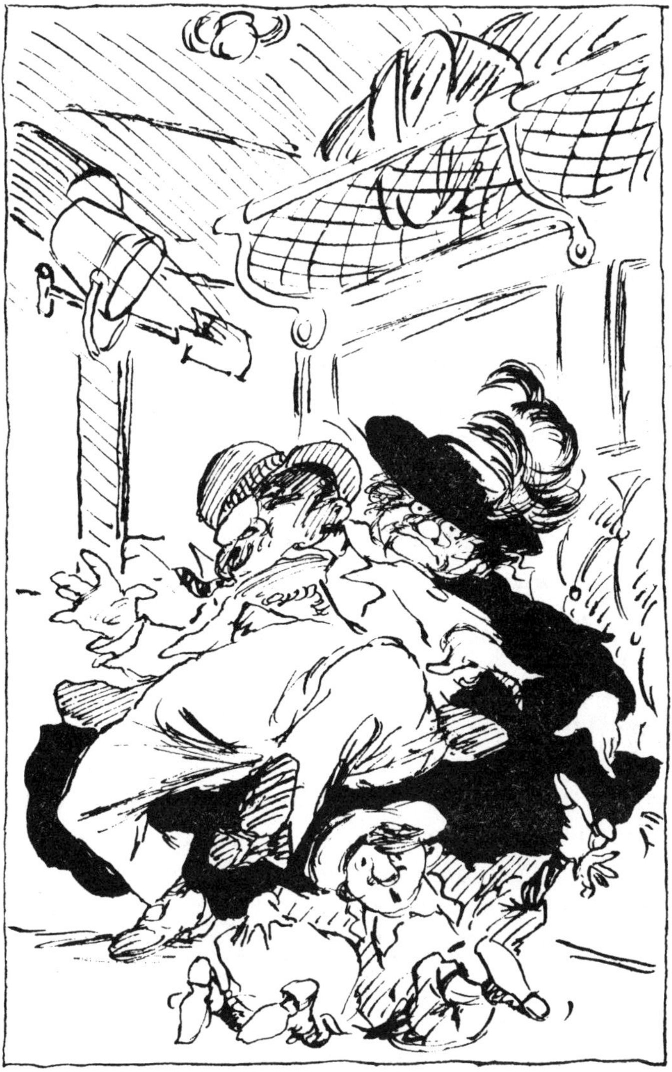

'ad me 'at on when our kid's spade and bucket fell on me.'

A voice hails Mr Buckle from the other side.

'Oi! There's a bloke down 'ere reckons some suffragette threw herself off a bridge in front of the train.'

'Damn woman ought to be locked up then!'

'More likely it's something to do with the signals,' shouts someone further down.

'No – it's the heat buckled the lines. You can take it from me. Hot metal expands and . . . well, it's always happening in India my brother says.'

'This ain't ruddy India!'

Up and down the train, the rumours and the speculations pass.

''Ere!' calls the man whom Mr Buckle first addressed. 'It's a kid! They say back 'ere it's a kid fallen out a carriage.'

'A *kid!*'

'It's a kid!'

'They say it's a kid!'

'*Look!* They're right!'

Beside the track, a guard and several passengers walk back towards the train. One man has a small child in his arms. Down the train, one question buzzes. Then . . . .

'It's all right! Talk about lucky! A bang on the 'ead, but he's all right, they think.'

'Bang on the 'ead! I know where I'd bang 'im if he was mine!'

'How did it happen?'

'What was his parents thinking of?'

Forever after, falling from the train is no longer a

remote improbable threat like the Bogeyman or Jack the Ripper. And when the younger Buckles are lectured about never, nohow meddling with the handles and the catches of railway carriage doors, they are always commanded to remember what happened to the little boy at Westcliff!

The excitement, after the first fright, has put most people into a good humour, and even Charlie is not impatient with the delay. And, when, with a whistle, the train moves off, everyone is busy gathering their possessions once again.

Charlie scrambles onto the seat to reach his rod down from the rack where he has stored it, and only just avoids poking Florrie in the eye.

'For goodness' sake, watch what you're doing!' all the family shout.

'What made Mr Culley go and give you the dratted thing for I'll never understand,' complains his mother. 'A man of his age ought to have learnt more sense.'

'No fool like an old fool!' is Aunt Ada's comment.

What he thinks about old Mr Culley, Charlie does not say; but he likes him better than he does Aunt Ada.

Having stood the precious rod for safety in the corner of the seat, Charlie climbs back to collect the jar of worms. His astonished yelp makes him the centre of attention yet again.

'It's me worms! The jar's tipped over and half of them is gone!'

All the ladies shudder, pluck at their skirts and search anxiously about them.

'Worms!' protests the fat lady to her husband.

'Imagine!'

But there is no trace of worms, neither on the seats nor on the floor. They must have fallen through the string mesh of the luggage rack; so where are they now?

Aunt Ada bends to flick away a speck of dust that dares to settle on her skirt, and, as she does, so a worm tumbles past her nose and wriggles at her feet.

'Your 'at, Ada!' roars Mr Buckle. 'They're in your 'at!'

Aunt Ada's hat is of stiff straw, shiny and navy blue, its shape like a hill encircled by a deep ditch or moat. Aunt Ada was sitting directly beneath the jar Charlie had stood most carefully on the rack, and, when the train stopped so suddenly, it must have been dislodged, and the worms have fallen down and now lie writhing inside the wall of that confining brim.

'Get 'em off me! Get 'em off me!'

Aunt Ada sits rigid – terrified to move in case more worms escape. Only her fingers fidget with her panic.

'Someone! Get 'em off me!'

'Keep yer 'air on!' Mr Buckle laughs. 'Looks like the live eel stall in there ... Cor, 'ere's a beauty!' And he holds a plump worm up for her inspection.

'Don't be disgusting, Albert!' says Mrs Buckle. 'Get rid of the 'orrid thing!'

'No don't, Dad!' cries Charlie, as his father makes to toss it through the open window. 'Put it in me jar. I'll need it.'

And so Mr Buckle picks worms from Aunt Ada's hat and drops them into Charlie's jar. When the last has been retrieved, Aunt Ada sinks back breathless, too exhausted by her ordeal to say all that she feels needs to be said. And the train pulls into Southend Station.

They have arrived.

Chapter 4

The only comfort Charlie can take from having been on the wrong side of the carriage for looking at the sea is that they are on the right side for getting off first. Just as soon as Mrs Buckle allows that they have stopped, Charlie has the door open. But getting their persons and belongings down onto the platform is not accomplished in a hurry, and the fat man and his wife and daughter have to wait behind them, breathing deeply and tutting with impatience. At last, Mr Buckle, Mrs Buckle and little Topsy, Aunt Ada, Florrie, Albert, Charlie, Minnie, their bags and baskets are caught up in the crowd which shuffles to the exit. Again Charlie and Minnie have to slip through on their own; but there are no mishaps this time and they join the family on the steps outside the station, ready to follow the procession making for the sea.

They pass beneath the railway bridge as a train rumbles overhead, and make their way along the High Street. Half of London's here, bent on having a good time regardless of the news.

'Yoohoo!' calls a lady with a feathered hat which nods rapidly as she speaks, like one of the pigeons pecking crumbs dropped on the pavement. 'Yoohoo! . . . Doris!'

On the other side of the road, Doris looks round and then shouts back: 'Hello, Gladdy! You get down here, too?'

'Yerse! I asks yer – all the way down 'ere and the first

thing you know you're meeting people from round the corner.'

'I know! Good job it's me old man I'm with. You couldn't keep nothing secret 'ere!'

''Ave a good time then! Don't do nothing I wouldn't!'

A tram drowns their laughter as it rattles along its lines like some amphibious ferry, the pilot standing in the bows controlling its progress with his bright brass levers. Both decks, below and the upper open are crammed with passengers eager for a ride along the sea front. Then, with a clanging of its bell, the tram slows before it runs down a cyclist whose front wheel has slipped into one if the grooved tram-rails and brought him tumbling to the ground. He scrambles to his feet and, swearing, drags his machine to safety, while onlookers cheer or laugh at him.

Very few people are walking *up* the High Street, away from the front; and these few, mainly locals, have to push through the eager crowds heading for the promenade and beach.

Charlie is scarcely able to contain himself when Mrs Buckle and Aunt Ada pause to look in windows and compare the prices with what was asked in Hackney. *Shopping!* Who would believe that anyone, even grown-ups, could waste precious moments on saucepans and flannel shirts when there were waves and sand to play with and fish waiting to be caught?

But, at long last, the High Street ends, and there, at the bottom of the Royal Hill, it lies – the sea. And, striding out into the estuary, the pier, over a mile long, with one of the new electric trains carrying trippers to the pierhead where paddle steamers berth. And, beyond that, on the far side of the Thames, like the coastline of a foreign land, the beaches and the fields of Kent.

Down the steep slope the Buckles' party troops, beneath the statue of Queen Victoria looking not at all amused as she points her subjects to the simple pleasures which a loyal resort can offer them. Already, other families stroll along the promenade. Sailing boats, drawn up by little jetties which run out into the sea on wheels, invite holiday-makers to take a trip around the pier; and donkeys plod up and down with children clinging to their saddles.

At the bottom, the Buckles cross the road and continue walking along the promenade until they reach that stretch of beach just past the gasworks the family always goes to, and which is handy for the lavatories. The children feel they cannot wait another moment to kick off their boots and socks and run wildly down the beach. And, then, their feet are actually on sand and shingle. In Indian file, with Mr Buckle at their head, they pick their way through other parties who have already marked out their territory with deckchairs and canvas windbreaks, until they find a spot considered to be satisfactory. Hiring deckchairs at tuppence a time is reckoned a waste of money, and Minnie and Charlie are put to work digging back-rests. The ladies declaring that they are dying of thirst, Mr Buckle and Albert are sent off to buy the day's first tray of teas.

Aunt Ada and Mrs Buckle, nursing little Topsy, are comfortably seated, propped against the mounds of sand the children have built up for them, when the men return, Albert carrying the teas and Mr Buckle with another paper tucked beneath his arm.

'Nothing really new,' he tells them. 'But I can't see it not happening now. You know, in a few days more it could be German battleships out there.'

Everyone gazes across the waves to where the pleasure boats are frisking in the sunshine and, beyond, the grey shape of a naval vessel steams out to sea. Mrs Buckle says that for two pins she'd pack up and go right now. And Charlie, in agony in case their trip should be abandoned, begs again for permission to go fishing.

'I keep telling you,' says Mr Buckle, 'it's no good down here on the beach. After we've had dinner, we'll all go on the pier and do it proper. The tide's coming in, so if you don't play on the beach now there won't be no beach left to play on at all.'

'All right,' Charlie bargains, 'so can't I get changed now and get on with it?'

Only Minnie and Charlie change. Florrie says she won't, not if she can't use a bathing tent. She'd die of shame if she had to change out here on the beach for everyone to see.

Screened on the shore side by Mrs Buckle's skirts, Charlie wriggles out of his trousers and pants and feels a playful breeze between his legs before he manages to step into his costume and pull the straps up over his shoulders. The coarse wool is scratchy, still stiff with salt from his dip last summer. He seizes his spade and bucket and scampers away down to the water's edge.

Rich mud oozes between his toes and the first wave running up the beach reaches out to cover and swirl about his feet. Charlie stands there, enjoying the sensation, gradually sinking up to his ankles until it looks as though he might be rooted there.

Minnie comes splashing down to join him.

'Mum says you're not to get wet yet. Only your feet.'

'But what's the use of a costume if you can't get wet?' Charlie argues. There are times, he thinks, when Mrs Buckle seems to lose her reason.

'Mum says you'll catch cold if you're in a wet costume for hours on end, so you can't get wet 'till she says.'

'Oh let's build a sandcastle!' Charlie mutters.

Together they labour, digging out a moat and heaping the wet and heavy sand into a tower. Then, while Minnie ornaments it with shells and bits of seaweed, Charlie excavates a channel so that with each wave the water floods into the moat and the castle walls begin to flake and melt away.

'Quick!' shouts Charlie. 'Dig! Build it up!'

Now the first wave breaks against the tower of sand and the children climb up on it, shrieking with excitement and clinging to each other for support. Suddenly, it seems to Charlie that the funniest thing in all the world would be to push Minnie over. It does not matter what may be the consequences; Minnie must be pushed. A quick shove and it is done. All in a second, Charlie sees her glee turn into astonishment; hears her happy squeals rise sharply to a full-mouthed scream; hears the splash as Minnie tumbles backwards in the scummy water; observes her vanish beneath a surging wave to reappear – as it hisses back – sprawling like some stranded sea beast on the sand. He hears her preliminary sobs; turns with the excuses already forming on his lips to face the outraged Mrs Buckle his conscience has created; slips himself and plunges headlong into the next wave which floods unstemmed over the vanquished castle. Charlie realises, with dismay, that he is *wet*.

Minnie has just recovered breath and prepares to renew her shrieks when again the tide engulfs her and she produces nothing but a gurgle. Charlie staggers to his feet, splashes over to his sister and hauls her upright. A 'rescue' might do something to appease Mrs Buckle, who is even now advancing down the beach. While he is actually in the water, Charlie knows himself safe from physical assault, for Mrs Buckle still has her shoes and stockings on. But, of course, he can't stay forever where he is.

'I think she's swallowed some water, Mum!' he calls.

'She'll swallow more if she goes on like that!' is all Mrs Buckle has to say. She has not witnessed, so it seems, how Minnie has come to swallow water in the first place. Neither – to Charlie's immense relief – does Mrs Buckle seem at all concerned that he himself has got wet without waiting for her say-so. It crosses Charlie's mind, as now and then it does, that it is hardly worthwhile doing as you are told; for, when you did, half the time no one remembered having told you to; and, half the time, when you didn't, no one remembered having told you not to!

Then Minnie is dragged off up the beach, and Charlie's left, king of the castle – except there is no castle any more.

The waves creep above his knees and inch slowly up his thighs. The sodden bathing costume sags and stretches. It might be decent, but is does not feel nice.

Charlie rouses himself. If it is all right to be wet, he ought not to stand here wasting time. He steps forward, out to sea. The water rises until it laps about his middle. He whirls his arms like windmills and is lost in a storm of spray. Stops, and a wave tickles his armpits as a strand of seaweed snakes round his chest. He picks it off and throws it from him. He looks back to the beach; sees the family still there and waves. Mr Buckle waves back to him and makes swimming motions.

Now, swimming on the bed at home is easy. Water

makes it much more difficult. Charlie goes through the actions with his arms.

'Lift yer feet up!' Mr Buckle bellows.

Charlie grins and half follows the instructions. That is to say, he takes one foot off the bottom and hops the next few strokes.

'Come on,' says Mr Buckle to his wife. 'Let's have a bit of a paddle. Can't come to the seaside and not put your feet in the briny. Give us a bit of appetite for dinner . . . You coming, Ada?'

'I don't hardly think so,' says Aunt Ada primly. 'All those years with her Ladyship I never took my stockings off in public, and I wouldn't care to lower myself now she's gone. Anyhow, one of us has got to stay with Topsy.'

'Oh, do come, Ada,' says Mrs Buckle. 'We can take Topsy with us.'

But there is no persuading her. And so, while Mrs Buckle struggles under her skirt with garters, and Mr Buckle unlaces his boots, Aunt Ada remains sitting stiffly where she is, loyal to the memory of her late employer and not a little like the marble Queen up there on Royal Hill. Neither will young Albert join the paddlers, but moodily throws stones at Minnie's spade.

Mr Buckle, Mrs Buckle, Florrie and Minnie pick their way down to where Charlie is now playing in the shallows.

'Ah, this'll do your plates a bit of good!' laughs Mr Buckle, as he and Mrs Buckle stand ankle deep in water.

Florrie and her mother hold their skirts up and beg Charlie not to splash them. Minnie in her bathing costume stomps about bad-temperedly.

''Ow's it going, Charlie?' Mr Buckle calls. 'Look, let yourself float on the water. You can't go under 'ere; it ain't deep enough.'

'Like this?' gasps Charlie, just as a wave breaks over his head and he staggers up coughing and gasping.

As the waves advance, Mrs Buckle and Florrie retreat, pulling their skirts up even higher, and Mr Buckle roars at their alarm and sings:

'Fancy seeing Mother with her legs all bare
Paddling in the fountains in Trafalgar Square.'

Their laughter is silenced by three deep bangs which shake the air like distant thunder. Up and down the beach, heads turn, all with the same question.

'Bert, whatever's that?' asks Mrs Buckle.

'It'll be the range out at Shoebury Barracks,' he tells her. 'Must be gun practice.'

'You don't think . . . ?'

'No, of course not!' he says. 'I tell you, it's just a practice, routine like.'

So taken up is everybody with the guns, that for a moment they forget the waves, and when they do notice the extra big one rolling in towards them it is too late. Before they can escape they are up to their knees in foam and water. The hems of skirts and petticoats are drenched; even the bottoms of Mr Buckle's trousers are soaked. Mrs Buckle and Florrie scuttle up the beach trying to shake the water from their clothes, with Mr Buckle and the children chasing after them.

And the great guns speak again.

Now, getting into a dry costume on a public beach is one thing. Getting out of a wet one, drying yourself and putting on your clothes again is quite another. Sheltering behind Mrs Buckle's skirts once more, Charlie wriggles free from the clinging costume; it rolls down his body and falls heavily about his ankles. Before his mother can wrap the towel about him, Mr Buckle begins his teasing.

'I see in the paper a man got fined here last week for changing on the beach. It's not permitted here, you know, after seven in the morning or before nine o'clock at night. I reckon if a policeman sees you like that, Charlie, he'll march you off as evidence.'

'Stop it, Bert,' says Mrs Buckle. 'He's only a kid. You're just trying to embarrass him.'

'Well,' says Mr Buckle, 'that's as may be. But, Charlie' – and he winks at him – 'if I was you, I'd keep me weather eye on the seagulls.'

'Why, what will the seagulls do?' asks Minnie.

'Never you mind, my girl,' says Aunt Ada, who is helping her niece into her drawers and petticoat. 'Some people ought to be a lot more careful what they say.'

'Yerse, they should!' says Mrs Buckle.

Mr Buckle groans. 'Cor, blimey!'

'Language!' Aunt Ada snaps; and Mr Buckle looks to the only other man, young Albert for support. But Albert still sits in sulky silence, the inside of his head echoing with 'language' which would have left Aunt Ada hairless.

Another problem about beach bathing is getting the

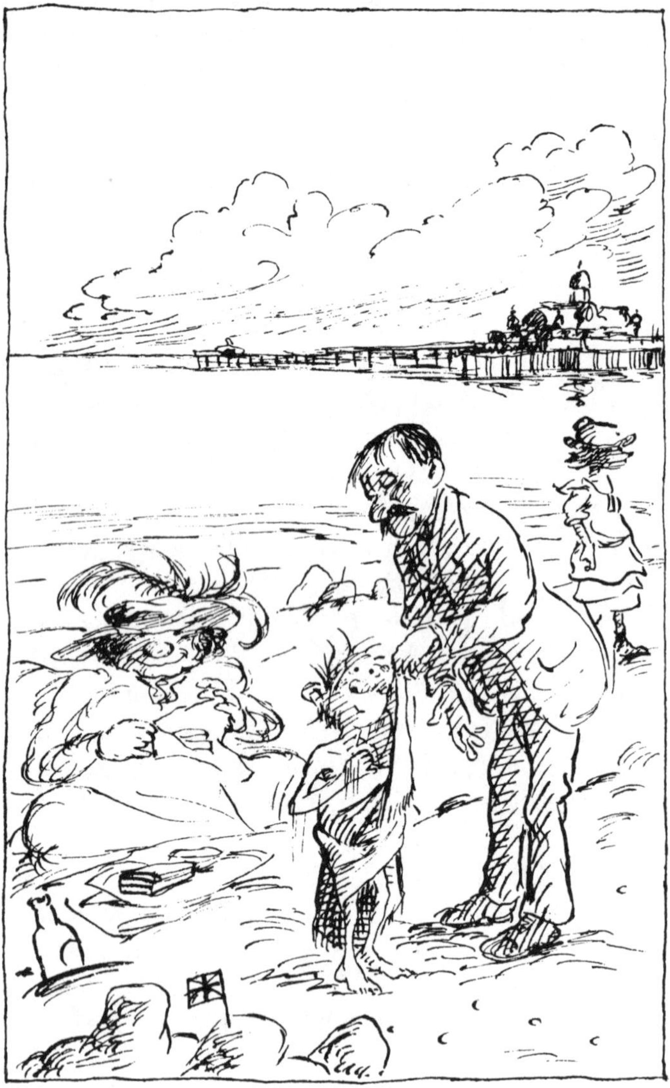

sand off your feet when you have done. And Charlie, when he is safely trousered, is sent down to bring back water to pour over feet that have to be held off the ground until they are dried and socks or stockings pulled on again.

Then it is found that little Topsy, who has been growing fractious, needs a change; and dinner is delayed until the soiled nappy is removed and hidden at the bottom of the baby's bag and Topsy has been reparcelled in a clean one. This operation has not dulled the family's appetite, and everyone tucks into the picnic with a will, even Aunt Ada, who regards most pleasures with suspicion. Sandwiches are munched: cheese and pickle, tomato and cucumber, jam and marmalade. And little Topsy, still too young to join in this feast, takes her refreshment at Mrs Buckle's breast.

Since the Buckles do not talk much while concentrating on their food, they all – for once – hear Minnie speak.

'Ain't the beach a *mess!*' she says, staring about her with half a sandwich in her hand. 'All them holes and castles. It ain't nice and smooth no more. We'll have to clear everybody off and turn it over.'

For a moment, the champing jaws are still as the family looks at Minnie in astonishment.

'Really!' Mrs Buckle laughs. 'What an idea! Eat your food up and stop talking nonsense.'

The meal continues, and as paper bags are emptied they are blown up and burst, all except the ones tomatoes have made soggy. It is not until the family is happily eating apples and sucking oranges that the wasps, which have been cruising round, begin to be really troublesome. Attracted by the sweetness, they zoom closer, circle menacingly and make to settle on hands and lips that drip with juice. So, what has been a peaceful and contented company is changed into a nervous, arm-waving, twitching party, any one of which may lose his nerve at any minute.

Florrie is the first to break. A wasp settles on her hand, folds its wings and begins to explore her sticky fingers. With a scream, she flings her orange from her, leaps to her feet and runs blindly off, trips and sprawls headlong in the middle of another family close by that is likewise engaged in emptying bags and filling stomachs.

"Ere, 'ere, 'ere!' cries the father. "Old yer 'orses!'

'It'll sting me! It'll sting me!' Florrie squeals, flapping the hand to which the wasp still gamely clings.

'It will if you don't keep still,' the man says, and grasps her wrist. He then flicks the wasp from her, picks up a rolled newspaper he has by him for the purpose, and smashes it down upon the insect as it lies struggling in the sand. 'Wopses is a real nuisance, but it don't do to get worked up. Only gets 'em mad, the nasty little beasts.'

'Thank you ever so,' sniffs Florrie. 'I just can't stand 'em on me.'

'I know, dear,' says the mother. 'I'm just the same.'

'*Her*! She panics if she sees a ladybird!' her husband says.

Florrie, who likes ladybirds, manages to smile.

Meanwhile, Mr and Mrs Buckle have hurried over.

'Sorry, mate,' apologises Mr Buckle. 'But you know what girls is like.'

'Silly child!' scolds Mrs Buckle. 'Have you thanked the gentleman?'

'Oh, don't mention it,' replies the man. 'Our Stanley here's no hero when it comes to wasps.'

'Mind you,' his mother says, 'he is unlucky. He's been stung three times already this summer. Ain't you, Stanley?'

Stanley, a youth a year or so older than Florrie, blushes, ashamed of being scared of wasps but half proud of being stung so often.

'Seven times last year,' he mutters, and glances at Florrie to see what impression this has made on her. Her round eyes satisfy him.

'Not surprised he doesn't like them,' Mrs Buckle says.

'Perhaps he makes them angry,' says Mr Buckle helpfully. 'If he starts flapping around as soon as he sees 'em, it could get 'em all worked up like.'

Stanley's dad agrees with him.

'Could be. Mind you, he's got an aunt they goes for just the same. Might be something in 'is blood they fancies.'

Stanley, sweating beneath the curious stares, pokes at the glasses which keep slipping down his nose.

'Heredity,' he says.

'What!' exclaims Aunt Ada – for the whole Buckle party except for Albert has followed Florrie. 'What!' she exclaims, suspecting she has heard a swearword.

'Heredity,' Stanley says again. 'Means it's been passed on.'

Aunt Ada sniffs. She approves no more of the young instructing their elders than she does of swearing.

But Charlie's not at all surprised by Stanley's language. Everybody knows that kids who wear glasses are always brainy. Not Arthur Nudge, of course, who couldn't learn to read but who could knock the daylights out of anyone who dared to tease him.

It is Florrie's voice which shrieks in warning.

'Look out! There's one crawling up your collar!'

Stanley springs to his feet, hands beating frantically about his neck. Then a yelp of agony proclaims the season's total now stands at four. As Stanley sinks down to the sand again, his mother falls on him.

'Get the sting out,' advises Mr Buckle.

'Have you got any tweezers?' Mrs Buckle asks.

'The wasp don't leave no sting!' gasps Stanley – a scholar even in affliction.

'Cold tea,' Aunt Ada says. 'Soak a hanky in cold tea and it'll draw the inflammation.'

It seems this is a remedy which has not been tried before. The teapot from the Buckles' tray is brought and, a handkerchief being found, it is dipped in the dregs. These are still lukewarm, but, in the circumstances, have to do.

As Stanley presses the hanky to his neck and tries to impress Florrie with his silence while enduring pain – it's too late now to do anything about that yelp – the grown-ups settle down to the pleasures of conversing with their new acquaintances.

The men, at once, begin a discussion of the news, and Mr Buckle learns that the soldiers at Shoebury have all been confined to barracks in readiness for anything that may happen.

'Yes,' says Stanley's father, who has introduced himself as Alfred Minchin, 'and I was at the bandstand earlier and there's this notice saying the military band from Chatham ain't going to play.'

'Shame!' says Mr Buckle. 'I like a military band.'

'But it shows how serious things is,' says Mr Minchin, 'when even bandsmen can't be spared.'

At this point, Mrs Buckle interrupts.

'Well, I never, Bert! These people live three doors from our Sophy over in Homerton. Know her well, they do.'

This coincidence is exciting and there's a feeling in the air that there is more to it than the chance encounter of strangers on a beach. Rather it is like the discovery of long-lost neighbours who have a lot of family gossip to catch up on.

Stanley, his parents say, has a good job in the Post Office. He's been there for a year and is doing very well. And when the Minchins learn that Florrie is to start next day making ladies' underwear the usual jokes are trotted out.

'But you're quite right,' says Mrs Minchin, when the laughter dies. 'A girl that's learnt to be handy with a needle and can manage a machine has got a trade that will always stand her in good stead.'

'Mind you,' Mr Minchin adds, 'you wouldn't have said that a few years ago. Sweated labour, that's what it was for them girls until the Government done something about it.'

'It's still not all that good for a lot of them,' says Mr Buckle. 'You can still find plenty of poky holes in Whitechapel. But it's not a bad little factory our Florrie's going to.'

'It's not right!' says Aunt Ada.

'What ain't?' asks Mrs Buckle.

'Governments telling people how to run their businesses. How much they've got to pay their workers. How many hours they can work them. How many they can put into a room. Never heard such nonsense! If people don't like the jobs, why'd they take them, just you tell me that!'

'Because there ain't no other jobs,' says Mr Buckle.

'So beggars can't be choosers.'

'But it's justice, woman!' Mr Buckle tells her. 'Someone who does a good day's work deserves a good day's pay!'

'I can think of plenty who don't know what a day's work is,' Aunt Ada sniffs. 'And I'll thank you not to "woman" *me*.'

'And who are you getting at then?' demands Mr Buckle. 'Come on, out with it!'

'A cup of tea,' says Mrs Minchin. 'I'm sure another cup wouldn't do us any harm.'

'You've taken the words out of my mouth,' declares Mrs Buckle. 'Albert, fetch us all another tray.'

'I'll come with you,' says Mr Minchin. 'You'll excuse us, ladies?'

Darting a final glare at Ada, Mr Buckle allows

himself to be led away by Mr Minchin, to get the teas and let his temper cool.

'It's a pity about your Florrie's freckles,' observes Mrs Minchin to Mrs Buckle as they wait for the refreshments to be brought. 'The sun always brings them out like that?'

'Oh, she's a martyr to them,' says Mrs Buckle. 'Five minutes in the sun and there you are.'

'It's not so bad for a boy,' says Mrs Minchin, 'but it does spoil a girl's complexion. You've tried Lightfoot's Limewater Wash, have you?'

'Can't say as I have. Good is it?'

'Well, I've got a cousin what swears by it. Used to look as speckled as a raisin pudding, she did; but now her face is as clear as yours or mine – well, almost.'

And while Mrs Buckle asks for details of cost and application, Florrie bows her head, hoping to conceal her disfigurement from Stanley, who pokes his glasses up and peers at her with more curiosity than consideration for her feelings.

Albert, all this time, has been sitting apart, saying nothing and stubbing holes in the sand with the heel of his boot. And now, when she has exhausted Florrie's freckles, Mrs Minchin turns her thoughts to him.

'He's a quiet one, your eldest,' she informs Mrs Buckle. 'Mind you, our Stanley's not got much to say – not in company, at any rate.'

'Oh, he didn't used to be like this,' says Mrs Buckle. 'I think he's got to *that age*. Know what I mean?'

'Oh, you mean . . . ?'

'Yerse,' says Mrs Buckle. 'Rather be with a certain

party than with his own family.'

'Really!' says Mrs Minchin, and stares even harder at poor Albert. 'We've not had that trouble with our Stanley yet. I don't know what's worse really – your boys getting all moody and mysterious or worrying about your girls being led up the garden path.'

Their conversation is carried on quite openly, and Albert, Stanley and Florrie dare not look each other in the eye. The returning of the men with trays of teas distracts the ladies and the conversation ends.

But now building castles and digging for buried treasure cannot keep Charlie's mind from the really important business of the day; and all the time the grown-ups sip their tea, he fidgets to be off and fishing.

'For goodness' sake!' snaps Mrs Buckle. 'We'll get no pleasure from this cup of tea if you're going to be a-grizzling and a-whining all the time. I'm sorry,' she apologises to the Minchins, 'but this old man he goes and visits gave him a fishing rod when he knew we was coming to Southend. And since then it's been nothing but fishing, fishing, fishing, morning, noon and night. I tell you, there've been times when I could've chopped his rod up for firewood, and that's the truth!'

'Used to fancy doing fishing myself,' says Mr Minchin. 'But I never got a rod like that. Going on the pier, are you?'

'Yes,' says Charlie. 'You catch the best ones off the pier. That's what Dad says.'

Mr Minchin agrees; but he looks more doubtful when he sees the jar of garden worms. For one thing, they don't seem to have much wriggle left.

But Charlie has a more powerful ally than Mr Minchin in getting everybody on the move. If the tide did not delay its progress for King Canute, it is certainly not going to wait for Mrs Buckle and a cup of tea. For some time, people who have settled closer to the water's edge have been forced to seek higher ground, so that the last few yards of beach are packed with trippers. And now the waves are only a few paces off and advance with every splash. Hastily, the two families strike camp and retreat up the steps to the safety of the promenade.

Chapter 5

The tide having driven them from the beach, the crowds in search of other pastimes amble across the road to the Kursaal Amusement Park where this summer you can ride on 'The Whirlpools – the Craze of the Continent', or see a film lecture, 'With Captain Scott in the Antarctic'. Both these attractions cost money, and the Minchins and the Buckles keep on moving in the direction of the pier, the bandstand and the Cliff Gardens with their promise of inexpensive entertainment.

From the little jetties, motorboats and sailing boats ply for trade, and bare-footed crews help giggling ladies on board while their children scream and dodge under booms and over thwarts to secure the best seats in the bows, impatient for the next trip round the pier to start.

Charlie looks at them with envy. He thinks again of Uncle Jack who promised he would take them on one; but he keeps quiet. He's anxious for his fishing and he doesn't want to risk losing that by grizzling for something else as well.

Minnie could not care less about his fishing, and she's got it in her head that she wants a boat ride.

'No, you can't,' says Mrs Buckle.

'Why not?'

'Because!'

'There's lots of kids going on boats.'

'You're not one of them.'

"'Snot fair!'

'Don't you start that, young lady.'

'Why can't we go?'

'Because it's too much money; because you've just had your dinners; because your sister's been sick already once today.'

'Oh, Mum!' says Florrie. It was bad enough having her freckles pointed out with Stanley gawping at her, without filling his head with a picture of her vomiting from a railway carriage window. But Mrs Buckle is already confiding further details to Mrs Minchin.

'That's how she lost 'er 'at. Didn't have time to get it off. Only just got her head out of the window as it was. Shame, a new straw it was, with these little flowers that almost matched her eyes. Oh, yerse, it's regular with 'er, always has been. And yet, somehow, it always comes as a surprise, don't it? I mean, you'd think we'd have put her by a window with her 'at already off. But there's the little ones, of course, always grizzling to have the window seats. No, Minnie Buckle! I've told you, you ain't going on no boat, and if the wind changes when you're pulling a face like that, it'll stay like it. It's funny with our Florrie; she always manages to bring up twice what she's put down . . . .'

Florrie feels sick again – with embarrassment.

'Funny!' says Mrs Minchin. 'You could be talking about our Stanley, leastways, until this year. I think he's growing out of it, at last.'

'You don't mean . . . ?'

'Yes, sick as a dog, regular as clockwork. I took him to the doctor's, didn't I, and told him it didn't seem natural to be as sick as all that as regular as that; but he says, "Mrs Minchin," he says, "he'll probably grow out of it." And seems he has.'

First wasps and now travel sickness. Florrie feels that she and Stanley have more and more in common. She glances shyly at his face to see if there are any freckles there. Stanley, conscious of her furtive scrutiny, jabs his glasses back onto his nose.

''Ere, Mum!' says Charlie, tugging at his mother's skirts.

'What is it? Can't you see I'm talking? It's not boat rides, is it? I've just told Minnie . . . .'

'No, no,' says Charlie. 'It's them people . . . Look!'

'What people?'

'Them people in the train.'

'Where? Oh, so it is!'

The fat man, his wife and daughter and another couple occupy one of the seats that face the sea. The pawnbroker is puffing fiercely at a large cigar and talking in his usual public voice.

'... 'Course, I don't hold with foreigners at the best of times. But when you get some German handing you your meat and veg it's enough to put you off your grub. What's he even doing here at a time like this? That's what I wants to know. If he was any decent German, he'd be back off home, that's what I say. Up to no good, that's what I reckon, and I don't mind who knows it. Well, I'll tell you this, when I tips, I tips handsome – don't I, old girl? – but I never give this feller a brass farthing, not a brass farthing! Mind you, I looked after the wine waiter. They'll not call Archy Turnbull tight up there. But I made my point, see what I mean? Not that I know what a high-class place like the Palace Hotel's doing employing the likes of him! Hardly patriotic, I'd say. And if you was to ask me . . . .'

Nobody does ask him; nobody gets a chance to ask him, because he is telling them already. And, as the Minchins and the Buckles pass on their way, his voice can still be heard informing a yawning world what Archy Turnbull thinks, what Archy Turnbull did, what Archy Turnbull would do if it was up to him.

'I know it's not right,' says Mrs Buckle, 'but I can't help feeling a bit sorry for them.'

'Who?' asks Mrs Minchin.

'These Germans living over here. I mean, it must be an awful worry for them.'

'Why?'

'Wondering what'll happen to them; and then there's their families back in Germany. I know how I'd feel if my Bert was working in Germany and there was this war starting.'

'Well, I've no time for them,' declares Mrs Minchin. 'If they didn't go starting wars, they wouldn't have nothing to worry about.'

'Don't talk daft, missus!' says Mr Buckle, chipping in. 'No disrespect, mate,' he adds quickly for Mr Minchin's sake. 'But it's not poor old Fritz trying to make an honest living in Southend who's starting it. It's your Kaiser and the likes of him.'

'If that's the case,' responds Mrs Minchin stoutly, 'I'd give the Kaiser what; I would straight. I'd pull every feather out of 'is helmet!'

'That's right, old girl!' laughs Mr Minchin. 'She'd soon put him in his place.'

'I thought they was relations,' says Mrs Buckle. 'The Kaiser and our King.'

'So they are,' says Mr Buckle. 'Cousins, or something like it.'

'Then it don't seem hardly right . . . families having wars like that.'

'The old Queen wouldn't have stood for it!' It is Aunt Ada, eyes flashing, her jaw thrust forward like a battleship. 'She wouldn't have stood for any nonsense. She was the Kaiser's grandmother, see.'

'You're right, Miss Hackett,' Mr Minchin says. 'They do say the whole royal family's really German. Do you remember doing the Kings and Queens of England back in school? After the Charleses didn't they bring the next king from Germany? I know our old teacher told us we'd had a king who couldn't speak a word of English.'

It seems a disconcerting thought, and no one is inclined to take the subject further.

But they have only walked a few more steps in silence when Mrs Buckle cries: 'Where's our Albert?'

The grown-ups have been engrossed in their discussion; Minnie and Charlie absorbed in gazing at the sights; and Florrie and Stanley, walking a few paces behind are explaining why each prefers Lemonade and Ice cream which costs twopence or Sherbet and Water at only a halfpenny; so that no one has noticed that Albert is no longer trailing after them.

'Drat that boy!' says Mrs Buckle. 'He's been mooning round all day, and now where is he?'

'No consideration!' says Aunt Ada.

'Charlie, Minnie, have you seen him?'

'No, Mum.'

'What about you, Florrie? You were at the back there with Stanley.'

Florrie colours.

'No, Mum. He *was* 'ere.'

'Of course he *was*!' says Mrs Buckle. 'But where's he *now*?'

'Stop creating, Ruby,' Mr Buckle says. 'He's big enough to look after himself. I expect he's just popped off to see a man about a dog.'

'What's he want a dog for?' Minnie asks.

'Don't be stupid!' Charlie groans. 'There ain't no dog.'

77

'But Dad said there was this man.'

'There ain't no man neither. Don't you know nuffink?'

Mr Buckle is half right about the reason for Albert's disappearance. He has nipped into the gents, but not so much to answer any call of nature as to give the family the slip. And when he emerges they are out of sight. Freed from the burden of his loved ones, Albert tips his straw boater at a more jaunty angle, thrusts his hands deeper into his pockets, and saunters back in the direction of the Kursaal with the hope of adventures more to his taste than trudging up the pier to watch Charlie attempt to hook a fish. With Letty at his side it would be perfect. But Letty isn't, and, as he has already realised, there are other and more attractive girls about.

The pub next to the Kursaal is at its busiest. The tables outside are crowded with trippers drinking and laughing. The Buckles aren't teetotalers; they'll always get a drop of something from the off-licence for a family do; but Albert's never been inside a pub. Now, with money in his pocket, he feels the time has come to prove his independence. Trying hard to look as though he's thoroughly at home, he ventures into the public bar. The air is rich, like Christmas pudding, with the fumes of ale, and Albert blinks in the smoky gloom after the brightness of the sunshine. So many people! In a corner someone hammers a piano; tills ring; and the hyena squeals of women's laughter leave Albert flustered. He edges his way towards the bar, finds a gap and stands there waiting to be served. He waits a long time. Again and again, other voices claim the barmaid's ear, hands wave money with their orders until Albert almost gives up hope. At long last his desperate: 'Miss!' is noticed.

'Yes, what's yours, dear?'

'Pint, miss – please. Mild and bitter.'

He sips the froth to save spilling it and threads his way back into the daylight. Outside, glass in hand, confidence returns, and he begins to enjoy the picture of himself. His glances at the young girls sitting with their families grow bolder. There is one with brown ringlets he feels sure would go with him if she were on her own.

He stands his empty glass on a window ledge and steps back on the pavement, twice the man he was.

'It's old Albert!'

Old Albert turns, a touch unsteadily, to see Jack Perkins.

'What you been up to, Bertie-boy? Not been in the boozer, 'ave yer?'

Jack Perkins stands there with both arms round the waists of two smashing girls – well, not bad, at any rate.

'Just a quick one,' says Albert, carelessly.

'Ain't seen you for months,' says Jack. ''Ow yer keeping?'

'Not so bad,' says Albert. 'Mustn't grumble.'

'Down 'ere on yer own, then?'

'Er, sort of.'

'What d'yer mean, "sort of"?'

'Well, I don't expect to be on me own for long.'

This Albert says with long and knowing looks at the two girls who giggle. Albert had no idea that he could carry it off as easily as this.

'You old devil!' Jack says generously.

'You don't seem short of company yourself.'

'Ah, now there's a story there,' says Jack. 'There really ought to have been four of us – Maisie 'ere and me, and Edna and Fred Geary. Remember old Fred? Well, poor Fred's gone down with mumps – and very nasty that can be at our age – so I've got me hands full, as you can see. Very nice too, except I don't feel I can give both these beauties the attention they deserve. So I'd say it was a stroke of luck bumping into you like this.'

'Very happy to oblige,' says Albert, sweeping off his hat, and thinking to himself that the world, after all is a wonderful place in which things did happen as they ought.

Jack releases the Fred-less Edna and Albert winds his arm round the vacated waist. He's had a little practice with Letty, walking in Victoria Park; but Victoria Park on a Sunday afternoon wasn't as carefree as Southend with a pint inside you and a mate and his girl to laugh and joke with too. This is fun. Of course, there'll be an almighty row when he gets back to the family. But they didn't ought to have dragged him along with them, and Albert resolves to put them from his mind and make the most of Edna.

'There ain't no point hanging on round 'ere,' says Mr Buckle. 'Gawd knows where he's got to now. He'll turn up sooner or later. He knows we're catching the six o'clock, so if he don't find us before then, we'll meet him at the station.'

For fifteen minutes, with impatience smouldering, the Buckles and the Minchins have waited for Albert to return.

'I shan't have a moment's peace,' says Mrs Buckle, 'worrying where he is. He'd no business going off like that.'

'Oh, give over, Ruby, and let's get moving,' Mr Buckle says.

On they go again. Charlie looks down at the bathers who still crowd the remaining strip of sand beneath the promenade, or perch like clumsy seabirds on the groynes. A man is throwing stones into the water for his dog to fetch, but the dog – no fool – stands with his forepaws in the waves, barking for a buoyant stick or ball.

The pier to which they walk is like a black line drawn across the bottom of the sky, the pillars supporting it as precisely spaced as the fractions on a ruler.

As they approach the bottom of Royal Hill, they can hear the strains of 'Rule Britannia' being churned out on a barrel-organ. A crowd has gathered round, some people actually dancing in the street, as patriotic tune follows patriotic tune, each one greeted with cheers and clapping. Nearby, stands a man selling Union Jacks. A tray full of them hangs from his neck; they are stuck in his button holes like nosegays and stand in a brave circle round his hat band.

'Show the flag and shame the Kaiser!' he calls

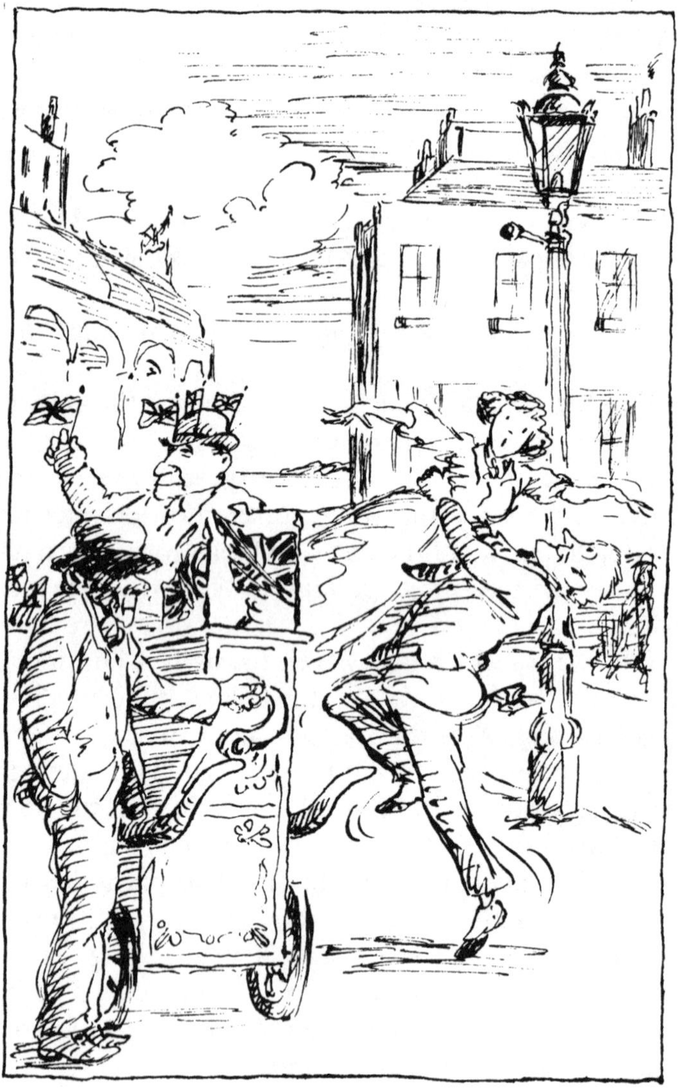

hoarsely. 'Tuppence to show you're British and you're proud of it!'

''Ere, let me treat the kids to one,' says Mr Minchin, and, in spite of Mr and Mrs Buckle's protests buys Minnie and Charlie a paper flag. 'And 'ave an ice cream, too. Let's all 'ave one, shall we?'

'That's ever so good of you,' says Mrs Buckle, as the children wave their flags and lick their penny ices. 'And what do you two say?'

Before the children can repeat their 'Thank yous', a man calls out above the din: ''Ere, look what's coming!'

A column of urchins marches down Royal Hill, some beating on tin drums, others sloping broomsticks like rifles, and all following the boy who proudly carries high a Union Jack and cries: 'Left . . . left . . . left-right-left . . . .'

'That's the spirit, lads!' the grown-ups encourage them.

'Show 'em what you're made of, boys!'

'Are we downhearted?'

'*No!*'

'Good old England!'

'Three cheers for King George!'

'Hip-hip hooray!'

Charlie is carried away by the excitement and makes to dart into the road and join the ragamuffin army, but Mrs Buckle holds him by the collar.

'Oh, Mum!'

'Just you stop 'ere. I'm not having you getting into no trouble.'

'But, Mum . . . .'

'No "buts", you're stopping 'ere.'

As the parade files past, the barrel-organ plays 'The Soldiers of the Queen', and, roaring out the words, people swarm into the roadway.

'Now then! Now then!' a deep voice booms. 'Move along there... *You*! Yes, you with the org*i*n,' the policeman says scornfully. 'That'll be enough of that. You're causing an obstruction.'

'Oh, come orf it, mate!' protests the organ-grinder. 'There's miles of room.'

'Move on, I said, or you'll be took in charge.'

'Oh, be reasonable, guv. Business ain't been as good as this since the old Queen's Jubilee.'

'Are you moving that contraption on, or are you coming down the station with me?'

'Oh,' the organ-grinder swears and stops cranking his instrument in the middle of the tune.

'Leave him alone! It's a free country, ain't it!' the crowd calls out, and hoots the policeman as he escorts the street musician up the hill.

Following this episode, the Buckles and the Minchins turn towards the entrance to the pier; and, at last, thinks Charlie, he is actually going to get a go at fishing.

''Ere, Bert,' says Mr Minchin (the men have already got on first name terms), 'do you think you'll be joining up?'

'Not me,' says Mr Buckle. 'This war's nothing to do with the likes of you and me.'

'Mmm,' says Mr Minchin doubtfully. 'But what if they brings in conscription like the papers say; suppose they calls you up? You'd have to go then, wouldn't you?'

'Can't see as they could make me,' Mr Buckle answers; but he speaks without his usual confidence.

The two men walk a while in silence.

'Still,' says Mr Minchin, 'you and me both, we're getting on a bit. It'll be the young ones they'll take first.' A thought strikes him. 'Thank gawd our Stanley's not sixteen! What about your Albert?'

'Albert? He'll not be eighteen for near enough two years. All this'll be over and forgotten afore he's old enough.'

'Albert Buckle, stop it!' Edna squeals as they come out of the Haunted House together. 'A girl has to watch herself when she's with you.'

'Has old Albert been taking liberties?' Jack Perkins calls, following with Maisie.

'I should just think he has! Leastways, he would have if I'd let him.'

'I wouldn't call a bit of a kiss a liberty,' smirks Albert.

'Shush!' says Edna. 'Everyone will hear!'

'It's all that fish what does it,' Jack laughs. 'Fishmongers is always passionate.'

'Well, don't you go near no fish then,' Maisie shrieks. 'You're bad enough already!'

'They're both awful,' Edna says, but makes no effort to dislodge the arm that has sneaked about her waist again.

'Well, where to now?' says Jack.

'Somewhere where it's nice and *light*,' says Edna.

'Let's go along the prom,' says Maisie.

'All right,' Jack bows. 'Your wish is our command. Ain't it, Albert?'

''Sright,' says Albert.

They leave the racket of the Kursaal and wander four abreast along the promenade. Rides, ice creams, and haunted houses have already taken most of Albert's spending money, and his heart sinks when Edna cries: 'Oh, let's all have our photos took!'

'Yerse, with our 'eads through them things,' Maisie says.

On the pavement a photographer has a screen with four figures painted on it and holes cut where the faces are.

'A splendid group you'd make, young ladies and gentlemen,' says the photographer, approaching them.

'And what could be more appropriate in these stirring times?'

'Oh, can we, Jack?' asks Maisie.

'What do you think, Albert?' Jack says.

'Well . . . ' says Albert.

'I'm getting a bit short meself,' Jack admits. 'But could we run to a copy for the girls?'

The two boys stand apart and count their money.

'All right, then?' says Jack.

'All right,' says Albert.

'Very good!' says the photographer. 'Now, if this gentleman stands here and the lady next to him . . . very good! And the other gentleman here and this lady next to him . . . Yes, very good, very good! There's no doubt the uniform's most becoming to the gentlemen . . . Now, smile please, while I count five . . . Ready? . . . One, two, three, four, five . . . Very good!'

He screws the brass cap back onto the lens, draws the glass plate from the camera and disappears, head and shoulders, with it into the little dark room he trundles round on pram wheels. A few minutes later, he emerges and hands the print to Jack and Albert.

The girls shriek at the picture of themselves in bonnets and bustled dresses, attended by a sailor and a soldier, above whose strapping shoulders the faces of the boys grin sheepishly.

Chapter 6

'Ride out and walk back, eh?' says Mr Buckle. 'Give our legs a bit of a rest like?'

Good idea! thinks Charlie, delighted to be spared the long tramp to the pierhead.

'Good idea!' says Mr Minchin. 'Does that suit you ladies?'

The ladies are entirely suited. Tickets are bought, and the Minchin-Buckle contingent finds itself at the front of the queue waiting for the next train to arrive.

Soon, it can be seen trundling down the pier. The pier trains are made up of three coaches, roofed but with no sides, and on the front is proudly painted:
SOUTHEND LOCAL BOARD
CROMPTON ELECTRIC
RAILWAY

The returning passengers are scarcely off before Charlie is scrambling to get a seat right up the front near the driver and on the side which is beside the sea rather than the walk-way.

'Now, you kids hold on tight,' warns Mrs Buckle. 'And, mind, you'll stay sitting down, Charlie.' She herself hugs Topsy tightly to her, who so squirms and wriggles that Mrs Buckle wonders if they shouldn't all give up the pier in case baby needs a change.

Give up the pier! Give up the fishing! Charlie can't believe his ears! He'd rather chop Topsy up for bait than not go fishing now!

Luckily, the driver has walked back down the

platform and taken his place at what is now the front. And, before Mrs Buckle can call off the expedition, the train has started on its journey to the pierhead.

Everyone's excited, and not just the children. Rumbling along in an electric train, high above the sea, is something of an adventure even for the regular visitors. People chatter; some laugh nervously. Passengers on the walk-way side wave to promenaders, who clutch at hats that the breeze which always blows out here tries hard to whisk away.

Behind them, holiday-makers on the beach dwindle to tiny specks and the buildings shrink to dolls' houses and still the train bears them out along that highway of wood and iron propped between the sky and water.

''Ere, mate,' a man bellows in the driver's ear, 'is it right some geezer got killed here the other week?'

'Yerse,' replies the driver.

'Well, what happened?' asks the first man.

'Working on the track, he was. One of the trains came off the metals and he got knocked into the sea. Poor bloke didn't stand a chance.'

'Blimey! Does that often happen?'

'Now, don't you go starting nothing,' says the driver. 'These trains have been running here since 1889, and that's the first real accident there's been. You're safer here than on the streets back there.'

Nevertheless, passengers who have overheard this conversation draw back into their seats.

Halfway along, the train slows, clatters over points and waits as the other train passes with its noisy load of trippers shoreward bound.

Then – all too soon it would have been for Charlie at any other time – the train is slowing and pulling into the pierhead station.

'Let them off first, if you please!' the guard calls to the waiting crowds. 'Hurry along there, ladies and gentlemen. We can't get the trains up and down fast enough today.'

''Ere I come with my little lot!' Mr Buckle shouts good humouredly. 'Now, buck up, Florrie, do!'

Florrie is standing at the platform's edge, gazing down between the rails at the restless sea below. There is no planking beneath the metals, and it seems perilously easy to plunge between them into the waves that toss and slap among the echoing stancheons far below.

'Oh!' she cries. 'Look down there!'

'Come away!' Mrs Buckle calls to Minnie, who runs to look where she is bidden. 'Just you hold on to Auntie's hand!'

But everyone does look at the dark waters beneath the pierhead, at the avenues of rusting pillars and the transoms festooned with ragged seaweed.

It is a relief to turn back to the sunny world above, where happy groups wander, laughing, about the deck, and gulls quarrel over scraps thrown to them or hang like Chinese kites high up in the cloudless sky.

At the same time as the Buckles and the Minchins are alighting at the pierhead, so the paddle steamer *Royal Sovereign*, recognised by her twin red funnels with black tops and two white bands, arrives from London, berthing here before taking the rest of her passengers on to Margate. Her siren whoops and, in answer to bells signalling reverse, the great paddle-wheels churn the water into foam. The boards shake as crowds hurry to get a better view of the vessel, bright with paint and polished brass, wonderfully alive with oiled limbs, panting steam, and billowing smoke like a gaudy buccaneer who puffs at two cigars.

When the *Royal Sovereign* casts off and sails away down the estuary, her paddles leaving a broad white track behind her, people on the pier settle down again to strolling, paying pennies to see 'What the Butler Saw', or lolling in the deckchairs that line the sun deck. And yet others settle to the serious business of fishing. Each angler's pitch is littered with dismembered crabs and starfish. It is hard for Charlie to find a vacant spot, and when he does the family stands round to watch and offer their advice. Charlie, who has never fished before, does not want advice, and to be fair no one who tries to tell him what to do has done much more himself.

First the rod has to be taken from its bag and the sections screwed together, the reel fixed in place, and the line run through the rings. Then the strange wire gallows from which the sea-angler suspends his hooks has to be tied on.

'For gawd's sake, watch what you're a-doing of!' cries Mrs Buckle. 'You'll have someone's eyes on them 'ooks if you're not careful!'

The circle of spectators widens as the hooks swing alarmingly with every movement of the rod.

'Give's 'ere,' says Mr Buckle.

''S'all right!' Charlie breathes. 'I can manage.' And, in snatching the rod out of his father's reach, sends the hooks whirling within an inch of Aunt Ada's hat.

'Oh, take it orf him, do!' Mrs Buckle squawks. 'He'll do a mischief with it, I just know he will!'

And now Charlie tries to skewer some lifeless worms with the wicked hooks.

Florrie says watching makes her feel all 'orrible.

Minnie, almost in tears, declares that it is cruel.

'All right,' says Mr Buckle, when the vermicular corpse is dangling from the line, 'we're about ready to make a cast... Now, see that man, Charlie? Watch him. See 'ow he does it?'

The angler Mr Buckle points to has his hooks baited and prepares to make a cast. He swings the rod back

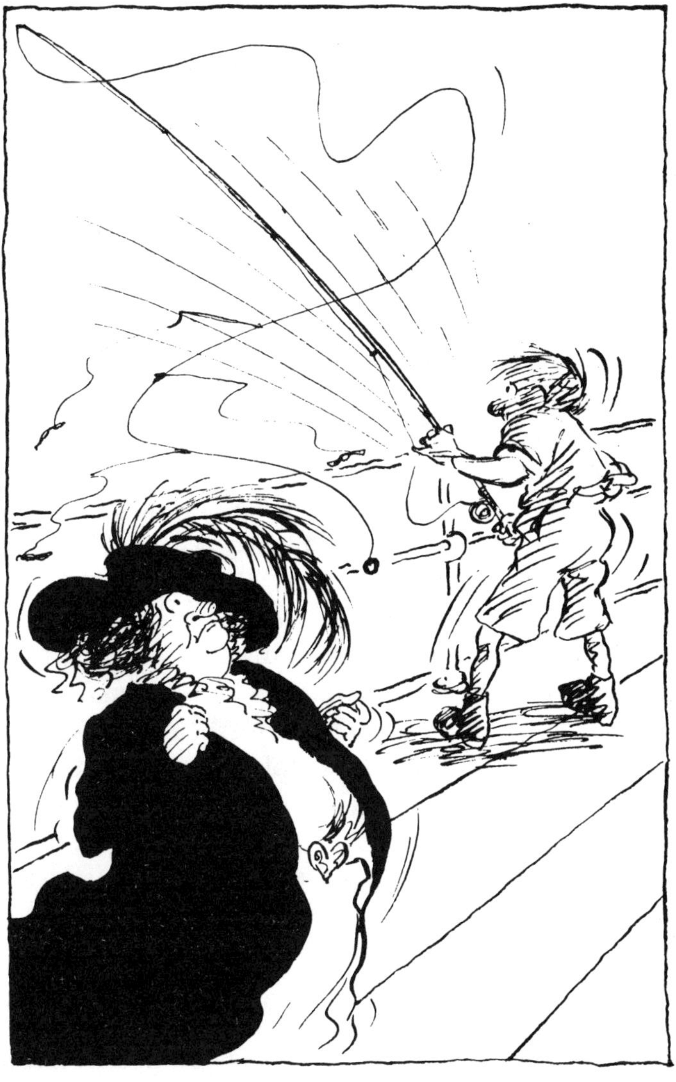

gently, then swiftly brings it over. His line, heavy with lead weights, flies into the air, up and out over the sea until it falls into the water. The shrill whine of the reel is silenced as though a giant mosquito has settled for a moment; and the man winds his line back with a pleasant clicking until it stretches tautly from the tip of the rod down almost invisible to the turbid waves. Every eye strains to follow the line to that world where sea creatures even now are gliding and darting as they hunt their prey: garfish, mackerel, mullet, plaice, flounders, eels. And at any moment, one might snatch at a tempting morsel and find itself dragged gasping and struggling helplessly into the dreadful empty air.

'Right, Charlie,' says Mr Buckle. 'Now you try and do the same – but keep a-hold of your line as you swing it back or you'll really give your mother something to create about.'

Charlie swings the rod back and then tries to whip it over as he has seen the angler do. It is only his first attempt. His line does not soar gracefully from the rod, but just drops into the water. Nevertheless, the baited hooks are down and Charlie makes haste to wind the slack in. The next job will be to land his fish. He grips the rod expectantly. There'll be a tug. Then he must jerk the rod smartly up to drive the barb into the fish's mouth. He must hold on tightly: a big fish could pull the tackle from his hands.

The rest of the party look down into the water, waiting. It is not five minutes before Minnie asks: 'Well, when's he going to catch this fish? Can't I have a go?' she adds when no one bothers to reply. 'P'raps I'll get one.'

'No!' snaps Charlie, anxious lest the grown-ups tell him to let Minnie have a turn just to keep her quiet. 'You don't know how to do it.'

'Well, you've not done it yet,' she retorts. 'You've not caught no fish.'

'Blimey! I've just started, ain't I!' Charlie reasons with her. 'That man there ain't caught nothing neither, and he started first.'

But, as if to prove Minnie's point, the top of their neighbour's rod begins to jerk and the little bell attached to it tinkles its alarm. Everyone watches breathlessly as the man begins to reel his line in.

'It's a whopper!' Stanley cries when, threshing and writhing, the fish breaks the surface.

The one person who seems quite unmoved is the fisherman himself, who winds his catch up deliberately, without any haste. It is a bass, a good eighteen inches long, rough of skin, black and white and scaly. He holds it firmly behind the gills to work the hook out of its mouth, then drops the creature in a basket where it flaps and gasps its life away.

Interest in the bass is still running high when a shout from Charlie brings them all crowding back to him.

'I've got one! I think I've got one!'

'Steady now!' cries Mr Buckle. 'Steady does it!'

As Charlie turns the handle of the reel, all eyes are fixed to the spot where the line disappears into the water. Inch by inch, the hooks are drawn closer to the surface – and here they come! But there is no splashing, no wild jerking; nothing but a limp strand of dripping seaweed. It is very disappointing.

'Never mind,' says Mr Buckle. 'Bring it up so's we can check the hooks is baited.'

Charlie swings his catch over the rails and wraps the weed round Minnie's face.

'Well, she's always in the way,' Charlie grumbles when Minnie has been dried and told crossly to stop her caterwauling.

The worms have gone from the other hooks, and Charlie begins to rummage in his jam jar for good replacements. The man who has caught the bass has been watching Charlie's difficulties with kind amusement, and now he leaves his rod propped against the rails and comes over to him.

'I don't think no one's ever caught anything with garden worms out here. You'd better try a few of mine.'

From the tin he carries, he pulls a lug-worm, long, thick as a sausage, slimy.

'Let me show you how we put 'em on.'

He takes one of Charlie's hooks and sticks the point into one end of the worm. Red and yellow fluid spirts from it, staining the man's fingers like nicotine. He keeps on pushing the worm so that he threads it onto the fishing line with the hook hidden at its bottom end.

'Right now, George,' he says, 'do you think you could manage one?'

'Yes!' says Charlie eagerly.

The lug-worm is wriggling and squashy as he picks it up, and, as he drives the hook into its head, it squirms, and Charlie's hands drip red and yellow, too.

Florrie shudders.

'Oh, it's horrible! I can't bear to watch it, I really can't!'

Stanley seems to choke before he says: 'Shall we have a bit of a look round the pier then?'

'Oh!' says Florrie. 'Oh! Well, if you like ... Is that all right, Mum?'

'What?' asks Mrs Buckle.

'Me and Stanley have a bit of a look round the pier?'

'Yerse, but don't get lorst ... It's enough with Albert wandering off on 'is own like that.'

'I'll come,' says Minnie. 'Fishing's boring.'

'Well, just you stay close to Florrie, then, young lady,' Mrs Buckle orders. 'And for gawd's sake don't go falling off the edge!'

No one notices the frown crease Stanley's brow when Minnie volunteers her company. But he says nothing, and so, with Minnie running on ahead or hanging back to look at something, he and Florrie begin a promenade of the sun-deck.

Charlie, having strung his hooks with lug-worms, prepares to make his second cast. He does better this time, and the baited line sails out quite a way before plummeting into the water.

'Well done, George!' the angler congratulates him, and goes back to keep watch by his own rod.

'Thanks, mate!' calls Mr Buckle.

Aunt Ada sniffs.

'Some people can't stop interfering!'

'Interfering, Ada!' Mrs Buckle says. 'I think it was very nice of the gentleman. There's those as wouldn't bother to help a kid like that.'

'And there are those as are able to look after their own kids,' says Aunt Ada.

'Oh, now you're not being fair!' cries Mrs Buckle. 'Albert's no fisherman, and no reason why he should be.'

'I don't know about you ladies,' Mrs Minchin breaks in tactfully, 'but I could do with a sit down. Suppose us girls leave the men to it and give our feet a rest. It's a long walk back, you know.'

'Yerse, you do that,' Mr Minchin adds. 'We'll come and tell you if young Charlie lands a whale.'

Aunt Ada does not much care for being organised by strangers, but neither does she want to stand any longer waiting for her nephew to get a bite; and so the three ladies go off to find a sheltered corner where they can sit in comfort for a while.

Florrie and Stanley visit the life boat; they look at the posters for the Jolly Boys' Concert Party; they watch the big ships steaming down the estuary from London and the Tilbury Docks. But none of these subjects has them chatting as easily as they have done before. Florrie fills all the gaps in conversation by asking: 'Where's Minnie got to now?' And Stanley, growing restless with her sisterly concern, behaves like a man with something weighty on his mind.

They have paused by a machine which promises to tell your fortune if you put a penny in the slot, and Florrie is saying for the fiftieth time: 'I wonder where . . . ?' when Stanley, like a cuckoo popping from its house at one o'clock, has kissed her cheek. It is so quick that Florrie's mouth is still open, saying: '... Minnie can have got to?' and she almost doubts that it has really happened.

'Hope you don't mind,' Stanley mutters. He studies the instructions for getting his fortune told. 'You're a bit of all right, I think.'

It is true!

It did happen!

And he thinks she's a bit of all right – Florrie Buckle!

'Oh!' she croaks. 'No ... no, I don't mind.'

'A bit of all right.' Those were his words. A girl couldn't have anything nicer said to her. Florrie peeps shyly at him, standing there not daring to say more and poking those glasses back up his nose.

'I *saw* you!'

It is Minnie.

'I saw you *kissing*! I'm going to tell!'

Stanley gulps in guilty terror.

'I'm going to tell Mum!'

Minnie is one of those children who never misses anything which is not intended for their eyes.

'I'm going to tell Mum; you see if I don't!'

'Come here, Minnie,' Florrie says.

'No, I'm going to find Mum.'

'I said, *"Come here."*'

'Well, what is it?'

Florrie fixes Minnie with a look she has never seen before.

'Now, you listen to me, Minnie. You're not going to tell no one nothing.'

'Who says?'

'*I* says.'

'You can't stop me.'

'We'll see. Now you listen hard... If *you* tell, *I'm* going to tell.'

'Tell what?' asks Minnie, a crowd of half-forgotten misdeeds scampering back into her memory.

'Well, to start with who it was what broke Mum's favourite vase... Then there's the money you was given every week for Sunday School that never went in no collecting-bag; and, if that's not enough, then....'

'You wouldn't, Florrie?' Minnie whimpers.

'Oh, wouldn't I? You go running with your tales to Mum and you'll see just what I wouldn't!'

'It's not fair!'

Florrie ignores her whines.

'Stanley, I think it's time we went back now,' she says. 'Don't you?'

'Oh, yerse,' says Stanley. 'If you think so.'

'It don't seem possible, does it?' says Mr Minchin, as he leans with Mr Buckle against the railings, idly watching Charlie's line.

'What don't?' says Mr Buckle.

'Well, all this. I mean the sun shining, us 'ere on the end of the pier, the women snoozing in deckchairs, kids playing, your Albert off chasing the girls – leastways, that's what I reckon.'

'Me too!' laughs Mr Buckle.

'And somewhere there's people deciding whether to start a war or not.'

'And they won't ask the likes of you and me,' Mr Buckle growls.

'You know,' says Mr Minchin, 'the more you think about it the 'arder it is to make any sense. I mean, what's the purpose of it all? I've never heard of anyone being better off because there's been a war.'

'Not *us*, Jim. You might just get a medal not worth a tanner. There again, you might lose a leg, in which case they might give you two. But the geezers what makes the guns and the geezer what makes the medals, come to that, it ain't tanners or even bobs they'll be raking in – it'll be a fortune!'

'You really think so, Bert?'

'Stands to reason.'

The men continue gazing at the waves, which, drawn by the unseen moon, begin to ebb, carrying with them toy boats, balls, straw hats, wooden spades – a thousand odds and ends the tide has borne away.

'Did we ought to be making a move?' Mrs Buckle asks when with little Topsy, Mrs Minchin and Aunt Ada, she comes back to the fishermen.

'Any luck yet, Charlie?' Mrs Minchin says, peering down into the sea.

Charlie shakes his head.

'Well, Bert, are we going to go?' Mrs Buckle asks again.

'Oh, just a bit longer!' Charlie begs.

Mr Buckle looks at his watch.

'Could give it another ten minutes, I suppose.'

'It's a long walk back,' points out Mrs Buckle.

'Please, Mum!' Charlie pleads.

'Ten minutes won't make no difference,' Mr Buckle says.

Mrs Buckle allows ten minutes.

'And where's Florrie and the others got to?'

'Here they come,' says Mrs Minchin. 'Look, there! Ooh-ooh!' she calls.

Florrie waves back at her and Stanley smiles. Minnie stumps along, two steps behind them.

'We're almost going,' Mrs Minchin tells them. 'Just giving Charlie a last chance to catch his fish.'

'Oh, ain't he got one yet?' says Florrie.

'Said he wouldn't!' Minnie sneers.

'Shut up!' says Charlie.

Desperately, he grips his rod, ready to strike the instant that he feels a bite.

'No need for that, Minnie,' Mrs Buckle says. 'She been behaving, Florrie?'

'No fear of any mischief with my Stanley there to keep an eye on things,' Mrs Minchin boasts.

Minnie glares, but she catches Florrie's eye and keeps her mouth shut.

'Well, I really think it's time to make a move,' Aunt Ada says. 'What with the baby to hump and those children dawdling, it will take longer than you think.'

'You're most likely right,' says Mrs Buckle. 'Now, come on, Charlie. You've had a good long go, you know you 'ave.'

'Oh, Mum!'

'Better give it best, son,' Mr Buckle comforts him. 'We'll come down again, eh. Better luck next time!'

While the others gather up the bags once more, Charlie reels his line in. It is Mr Minchin who spots it first.

''Ere, Charlie!' he calls. 'You've got something there!'

His shout brings everybody hurrying to the rails. And there is something hanging from one of Charlie's hooks, something which feebly flaps from time to time. It isn't very large and only when Charlie swings his catch onto the deck can he see that it's a dab, not six inches long. But it's a fish, a real fish! And Charlie's caught it, no one else.

The friendly angler comes over to inspect it.

'My word, George,' he says. 'You don't often get a dab out here. Well done! Now, mind how you take the hook out of his mouth. You don't want to tear him, and you don't want to get hooked up yourself.'

Charlie holds the tiny flat fish affectionately. He feels grateful to it for getting caught on his line; and he's sad when it lies still. But nothing can spoil his sense of triumph. The dab is wrapped in newspaper so that he can take it home, and Mrs Buckle promises to cook it for him.

'Not that you'll get more than a mouthful off its bones,' she says.

There is probably nowhere else in Britain where you can walk along a highway that for a mile and a half is absolutely straight. As the family and their friends begin their journey back to land, the railings on either side and the railway lines all vanish at one distant point. The boards spring gently beneath their feet; their dwarf shadows keep step just in front of them; and the strong breeze claws at the ladies' hats and tries to lift their skirts. Only when they pass one of the shelters are they out of the wind and can feel again the warmth of the sun which still shines down and sparkles far beneath them.

In one of the little bays which jut out like balconies from the walk-way, Charlie comes across one of those telescopes you can look through for a minute if you put a penny in. Entrusting his rod and precious dab to other hands, he puts his penny in the slot. It's difficult to see anything at first, and then he realises that he is only looking at the waves. He points the telescope along the pier, and there before his eyes are the head and shoulders of a giantess. He sees her teeth like chunks of discoloured ivory and a finger, wrinkled like tree bark, scratches a nose, purple-veined and pitted. Charlie swings the telescope again, and people, railings, wrought-iron lamp-posts fly past until he finds a sailing boat tossing on the sea, its passengers laughing and chattering, but without a sound, like the moving pictures at the Electric Theatre he has sometimes seen. Then Charlie finds himself looking at a section of the promenade. Two young men, they aren't much more than boys, are sitting on a bench with two girls between them. The girls have obviously got the giggles as the boys squeeze them, whisper in their ears and kiss them. That boy on the left looks just like someone Charlie knows . . . .

'*Mum!*' he shrieks.

'My gawd!' cries Mrs Buckle. 'Whatever is it?'

'It's our Albert!'

''Ere, let me look!'

But, at that moment, there is a click as the shutter falls. And, by the time another penny is produced, and Charlie has found what he thinks might be the same place, there is no trace of amorous young men . . . still less of Albert.

'Are you sure?' Mrs Buckle asks, suspiciously.

'Yes, Mum,' says Charlie. 'There was two of them, and he was kissing this girl.'

'What did I say?' Aunt Ada sniffs.

'I'll give him kissing!' Mrs Buckle says.

Mrs Minchin is most sympathetic.

'It must be a worry for you, dear.'

This is all too much for Minnie. Never in her life has she had such a tale to tell. But Florrie holds her eye, and Minnie holds her tongue, while Stanley prays for someone to change the subject.

'Well, I only hope you'll have something to say when we get hold of him,' Mrs Buckle tells her husband. ''Ere! You don't think it was this Letty, do you? You don't think he arranged to meet her down here? Why, the deceitful, sly . . . !'

''Old on! 'Old on!' says Mr Buckle. 'Blimey! You don't even know if it was young Albert Charlie saw. In any case, where's the harm in it?'

'Harm!' Aunt Ada snorts. 'Some people don't ever learn.'

Mr Buckle rounds on her.

'And what does that mean, Ada?'

'Nothing.'

'Then you might as well keep quiet about it!'

'Now then . . . now then!' says Mrs Minchin. 'I'm fair famished. If I don't get a plate of cockles soon, I'll not get up that hill again.'

All this time, train loads of visitors have been trundling to and fro, the passengers waving and calling just as the young Buckles had done on their journey out. And, now, one train approaches them with a host of children on it, all armed with Union Jacks. They lean out of the carriages, clinging to the uprights, ignoring the adults who beg them to sit down, and wave their flags and cheer.

'Might be another paper when we get back,' says Mr Buckle.

'That'll be the third or fourth you've bought today,' his wife complains.

'You've got to know what's happening,' says Mr Buckle.

'Women,' observes Mr Minchin, 'don't really understand about this sort of thing.'

Mrs Buckle sighs.

'I don't know who enjoys all this war business most – the kids or grown-up men! 'Ere, what's the time now, Albert?'

Mr Buckle pulls the watch out from his waistcoat pocket.

'Almost half past four. We'd better buck up if we're to get these cockles before we catch the train. Best foot forward, everybody!'

Chapter 7

'Young man, watch where you're going, can't you!'

The lady in the bathchair swings her steering handle and narrowly misses running Albert down. The man bent double pushing her almost falls headlong at the unexpected turn.

'Ever so sorry,' Albert says. 'Just didn't see yer.'

The pekinese which sits wheezing at his mistress's feet yaps his own disapproval.

'You did ought to watch it, boy,' the bathchair-pusher scolds him wearily.

'Ooh! Albert!' Edna giggles.

'Cor!' Jack laughs. 'You nearly made the papers.

Just imagine the headlines: "Youth Struck Down by Bathchair... Victim of Reckless Granny."'

'Ooh!' squeals Maisie. 'The things you say!'

'I know! I'm famous for it!'

'Well,' says Albert, not wishing to let Jack hold the stage too long, 'how about a bit of the old tiddley-om-pom-pom?'

'Oh! You're *awful*! You really are!' cries Maisie.

'Whatever do you mean?' gasps Edna.

'The brass band,' Albert beams. 'Whatever did you think I meant?'

'Well, with you I don't know what to think,' says Edna.

'Think the worst,' says Jack, 'and then it won't be bad enough. That's right, ain't it, Albert?'

Albert winks.

'I ain't obliged to give evidence against meself... Well, what about it? Shall we go and listen to the band?'

'Why not?' says Maisie.

'Yerse, why not?' cries Edna. 'I like a bit of music.'

'Then perhaps we ought to give the band a miss,' says Jack.

'Oh!' Maisie pretends to scold him. 'Don't you never stop?'

'No, not even in me sleep!'

The girls giggle and the boys guffaw as they stroll towards the bandstand just beyond the entrance to the pier, and from which they can already hear the deep ompah of the tuba and the bray of trumpets.

'You've got a moustache growing, haven't you,

Albert?' Edna says, running a finger across his upper lip.

'Yerse,' says Albert.

'I like a man with a moustache,' says Edna. 'Look ... like that soldier's there.'

She is pointing to an officer who strides purposefully through the crowds carrying a brief case beneath his arm. His whiskers bristle thickly like a well-trimmed privet bush, and it requires a lot of imagination to picture Albert ever sporting one as luxuriant as that.

'And uniforms,' Edna sighs. 'I do like uniforms.'

'Then we'll enlist, ladies, just to please you; won't we, Albert?' Jack says.

Maisie laughs at them.

'You ain't old enough, either of you!'

'Soon will be,' Albert says without a smile. 'And then I will.'

'What – go for a soldier?' Edna asks.

'That's right.'

'What about your old man?' says Jack, puzzled by Albert's sudden change of mood. 'I thought he was all against that sort of thing.'

'*He* is,' Albert says.'*I* ain't!'

Jack is startled.

'You mean you'd really join the Army?'

'Tomorrow, if they'd have me.'

'You must be ever so brave,' says Edna.

Maisie says, 'I've got an uncle what joined the Army. He went out to fight in Africa. He got hurt in the leg and he can't walk now, except with crutches. He can't work neither, and you should hear my auntie going on about it.'

They have reached the fringes of the audience gathered round to hear Mr Seebold and his band give their second performance of the day. The programme consists of a medley of patriotic songs and marches which set people's feet a-tapping, their lips pursed in whistles; others sing or hum when the words escape them.

'Strewth!' says Albert. 'Is that the time?'

He looks at the clock perched on stilts above a thicket of wrought-iron, which sprouts from the bandstand roof.

''Alf past five,' says Jack. 'So what? It's early yet.'

Albert clears his throat uneasily.

'Well, I've got to... what I mean is, I've made arrangements to catch the six o'clock.'

'Oh, you're never going yet!' says Edna.

'Who are you meeting?' Jack asks.

'Oh... people.'

'Forget about them. We're having fun.'

'Can't do that... They've got me ticket.'

'You're never with your mum and dad!'

'No! 'Course not! It's people where I work. It's an outing from the shop.'

'Well, let's go with him then,' says Maisie.

'No, no! Don't do that,' Albert stammers. 'There's no need to spoil your day.'

'All sounds a bit suspicious-like to me,' says Jack. 'With a dark horse like you, I shouldn't wonder if there wasn't another woman somewhere.'

'Oh, there isn't, is there?' Edna cries.

'No,' says Albert. 'No. 'Course there ain't. 'Ere, let's walk round the other side; we might see better there.'

'Now, is it cockles for everyone?' asks Mr Buckle.

Little white dishes heaped with cockles line the counter of the shellfish stall, and Charlie, Minnie, Florrie and the adults take one and begin to sprinkle vinegar and pepper over them. Charlie shakes the bottle and douses his cockles until the vinegar overflows the dish. He loves vinegar, and his mouth almost dribbles with the juices that are flooding it. When he puts the bottle down, the man who runs the stall and who has been watching Charlie with the pained expression of one who feels unfair advantage has been taken of him, seizes the bottle and, without taking his eye from Charlie, plonks it down beyond his reach. But Charlie, now shaking such clouds of pepper from the cruet that it is a wonder that the cockles do not sneeze, is unaware of plonkings and expressions.

The cockles are good. Large, succulent, quite free of grit, fished only yesterday, washed and boiled and offered for the refreshment of the public. Charlie eats like a connoisseur. He studies each one he picks and squeezes its plumpness before popping it in his mouth and chews deliberately to release the flavour.

Minnie likes cockles too. But for Minnie to *enjoy* means *more*, and more ... and more! The rows of dishes piled high to tempt the customer are all too tempting. No sooner does she finish one dish, than her hand stretches out to take another.

'*Mum!*' hisses Florrie. 'Look!'

'Whatever is it this time? . . . *Oh, my gawd!*'

A dozen empty dishes stand in front of Minnie who gobbles on.

Still protesting that she has not finished, Minnie finds herself dragged from the shellfish stall and escorted smartly along the promenade until they feel that they are safe from any demands to pay for Minnie's blow-out.

'Whatever was you thinking of?' Mrs Buckle wants to know. 'You'd have cost us a fortune!'

'Twelve dishes!' Mrs Minchin marvels. 'It's a wonder she's not ill. Just think of it!' she begins to chuckle. 'Twelve dishes!'

'Twelve dishes!' Mr Minchin whistles. 'And then she says she hasn't finished!'

The giggles spread until everyone, even Auntie Ada, leans on each other for support and laughs and laughs.

'Stop it!' Mrs Buckle gasps, the tears pouring down her cheeks and soaking little Topsy's bonnet. 'People will think we're drunk!'

'Oh, dear!' groans Mr Buckle. 'That child'll be the ruin of me! Well, how about a last cup of tea before we catch the train?'

'Good idea,' says Mr Minchin. 'But watch young Minnie. If she can drink like what she eats! *Twelve dishes!* I asks yer!'

Charlie gulps his tea down. Drinking tea is pretty much a waste of time when what is left of a visit to the seaside can be measured in minutes. And so he leaves the others at the tea stall, drinking, chatting, still laughing about Minnie's cockles, and wanders onto one of the small jetties used by the pleasure boats to land their passengers. At its highest, the tide has covered it, and although it is now ebbing fast, it has left the planking wet and slippery. Charlie's rod is back in its case but he carries it and as he stands on the jetty's edge, he remembers his triumph out there on the pier, right out there in the middle of the estuary. Wait till Sidney sees his fish! Of course, he's bound to say it's titchy; but he'd still be jealous.

There'd be fish here too, thinks Charlie. Just down there are fish still swimming and feeding. He imagines his rod assembled and the hooks baited with juicy lugworms. He practises a cast, swings the rod backwards and then smartly whips it up and over. When he comes again, he'll know just what to do, and he'll catch big fish like that nice man's bass. You had to swing it back and then whip it up and over.

Charlie swings too hard. His foot slips and before he can cry out, he has fallen into the waves. The force of his practice cast is like a dive and he plunges head-first in. Water roars in his ears, stings his eyes, rushes up his nose and fills his mouth. Then, before he can float to the surface, a wave sweeps him between the wooden piers and underneath the jetty. Choking, desperately struggling to get his head above the water, Charlie does not have time to think that this is drowning, that this is what people feel just before they die, and that in a few moments more he will know nothing and never will know anything again.

Then something grips his arm and he struggles even harder to escape but cannot. It is dragging him, and no kicking or wriggling can free him. And then he is in the air again, spluttering, coughing, spitting and at the same time crying.

'You are all right,' a man says. His voice sounds odd. 'Now you will be all right.'

Other hands are reaching down to them.

'All right, mate, I've got him.'

'Lucky you saw him. What was he a-doing of?'

'Just wait till your ma sees you!'

Charlie is pulled onto the jetty where he lies, still spitting water from his lungs and trying to get his breath back. The next moment, it seems, Mr and Mrs Buckle are there, frightened, relieved, angry, all at once.

'Thanks, mate,' says Mr Buckle as Charlie's rescuer pulls himself out of the water. 'I dunno what to say.'

'No need to say anything. Already he recovers.'

The man's accent makes Mr Buckle start. He looks at him again. He is a man of about his own age. His moustache and close-cut hair are greying; the stiff collar and black tie he wears are limp, and the dress trousers with the silk stripe down the seams are sodden. His hands are white and soft, the nails carefully trimmed.

'You ain't English are you, mate?' says Mr Buckle. His voice sounds tight with his embarrassment.

'No,' the man answers wearily, 'I am not English ... I am German.'

The onlookers who have gathered to enjoy the excitement of a drowning fall silent for a moment, and then speak in whispers.

'Well... that was decent of you,' Mr Buckle says.

'You are surprised, I think.'

'No, no... not really.'

Mr Buckle feels in his pocket and pulls out half-a-crown.

'I'm sorry; I ain't got no more.'

The man looks at the coin in Mr Buckle's palm.

'Thank you, no. I accept tips only in the hotel when I serve meals. And now, please, you must excuse me.'

He gets to his feet and walks away.

'Thank you, everso!' Mrs Buckle calls after him.

The crowd stands aside to let the stranger pass; then, since the excitement is at an end, wander on their way.

'Makes you think, dunnit?' Mr Minchin says.

'He had to go right under the jetty to get your kid out. I ain't seen nothing like it. Straight in he went; didn't even stop to take his jacket off.'

'And it's not as though he's...' Mr Minchin falters. 'I mean, he's not even... well, you know.'

'I don't know why you're all making such a fuss,' Aunt Ada says. 'It's only what any Englishman would have done!'

Mrs Buckle, who is still comforting her son, turns on her. 'You don't think he was *interfering* then?... Not being *family*!'

It is Mrs Minchin who speaks first after the silence in which Aunt Ada has tightened her lips and resolved never to speak to her sister again, not unless she apologises, at any rate.

Mrs Minchin says: 'I wonder if he's got another suit. He won't be able to wear that one tonight. I shouldn't wonder if it's ruined what with the salt water and everything.'

The Buckles try not to think about the cost of a new suit, especially the posh sort that waiters wear. It is Florrie who draws attention to Charlie's predicament. What is Charlie going to wear?

'Right, young man,' says Mrs Buckle, 'you'll have to put your swimming costume back on until these clothes is dry. Come on, we ain't got any time to spare if we're going to catch that train.'

'But I can't, Mum!' Charlie cries, close to tears again. 'Everyone'll look at me.'

'If you don't wear it, they'll look even more. Come on! Let's have that jersey off you, quick now!'

Protest is useless. With people passing to and fro, Charlie is stripped and the damp and clinging swimming costume pulled on again.

Mr Buckle is just saying: 'Right, now let's get cracking . . .' when Charlie bursts into a violent fit of sobbing.

'It's no use crying,' Mrs Buckle snaps. 'It's your own fault if you've got to walk through the streets in your swimming costume.'

'It's not me cos-costume,' Charlie weeps. 'It's me fi-fishing rod!'

In all the terror of nearly drowning, and then in the fuss which followed, Charlie has not given a thought to the rod which caused him to lose his footing in the first place. When he tumbled in, the rod went in the water too. Where is it now? Floating out to sea, never to be found again? Charlie is more put out by losing it than by all the danger he's been in.

'You'll never find it now, Charlie,' says Mr Buckle, kindly. 'The tide will have carried it too far out.'

'Oh, please, let's have a look, Dad!' Charlie begs.

'Bert, we haven't got the time,' says Mrs Buckle.

'Oh we'll only be a minute,' Mr Buckle says. 'Come on, Charlie, but for gawd's sake, don't fall in again.'

Together they hurry down the jetty, with Mr Minchin and Stanley following, and gaze into the water for a sign of Charlie's rod. It is hopeless, and Charlie feels the grief like some choking lump stuck in his chest.

'I say . . . Hello, there!'

The call comes from a small sailing dinghy not far out.

'Is this what you're looking for?'

The man who has hailed them waves a fishing rod. Charlie hardly dares believe his luck.

'Yerse!' shouts back Mr Buckle. 'That's it!'

'Right-ho! I'll come alongside.'

The man speaks to a young lady who holds the tiller, and the boat tacks in the breeze and glides towards the jetty.

'Saw what happened,' the man says. 'Too far out to help, but spotted this.' He passes the rod up to Charlie.

'What d'you say, Charlie?' Mr Buckle says.

'Thanks, mister. Thanks very much!'

'Happy to oblige. All's well that ends well, what? . . . Right-ho, old thing, let's cast off.' And the little boat bobs out to sea again.

'Charlie,' says Mr Buckle, 'you've got the luck of the devil; do you know that?'

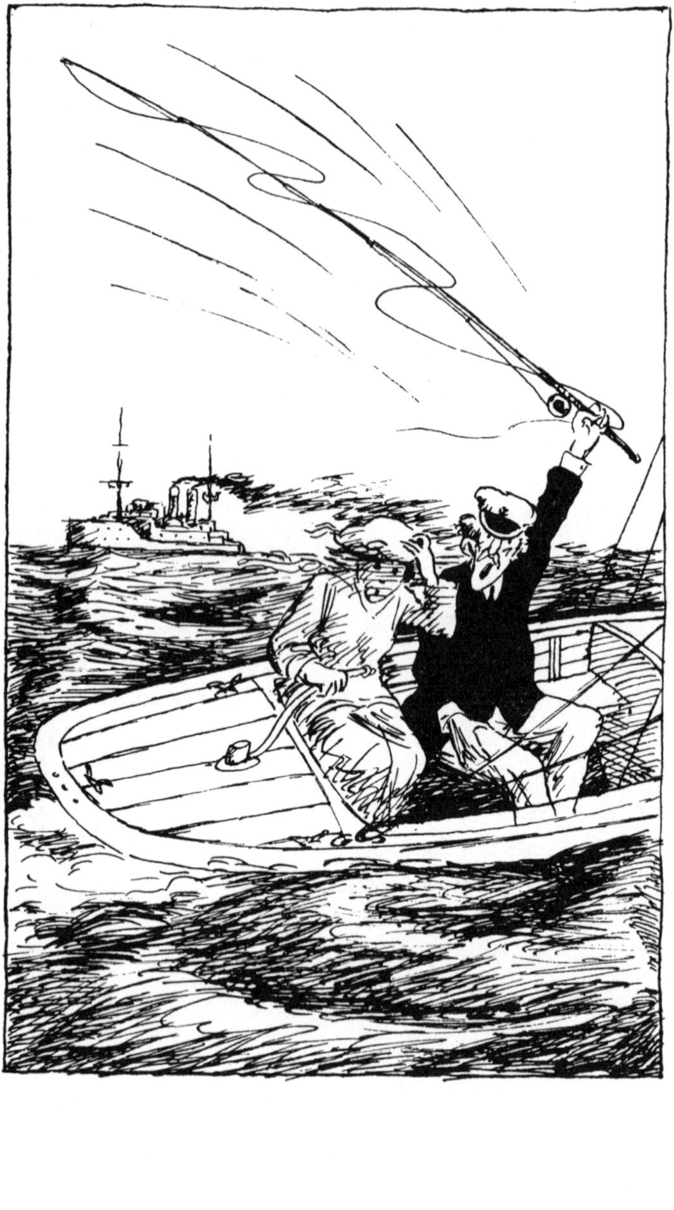

Charlie doesn't think that nearly drowning and nearly losing your fishing rod is very lucky; but he knows what Mr Buckle means.

'Now, come on, Bert!' Mrs Buckle scolds him. 'We're going to miss that train, and you know what a crush it is if you leave it later. 'Ere, you can hold 'is trousers.'

Charlie's socks and pants, jersey and trousers are being carried by members of the family and the Minchins to try to dry them as the party marches to the station. Charlie brings up the rear, ashamed to see his wardrobe fluttering like bedraggled flags for everyone to see. But even walking the streets in his swimming costume he carries his rod and fish in triumph.

'I'll really have to go now,' Albert says.

'Oh!' says Edna. 'What a pity!'

''Fraid it can't be 'elped,' says Albert. 'The train and the tickets – you know.'

'Yerse,' says Edna. 'Pity though.'

'Still, it's been a good day, ain't it?' Jack says.

'Ooh, ain't it just!' laughs Maisie.

'Not for poor old Fred,' says Albert.

'Oh '*im*!' says Edna.

'Ain't you missed him then?'

'Don't say I 'ave; don't say I 'aven't. Ain't you missed no one?'

'Not so's you'd notice.' Albert tightens his arm round Edna's waist. 'Give's a kiss, then.'

'What! In front of all these people?'

'Go on, Edna,' Jack calls out. 'Give 'im one. If he

runs off and joins the Army, you might never see him again.'

'Will I see you again?' asks Edna.

'Perhaps,' says Albert, dismissing a vision of Letty's grieving eyes. 'I'd like to.'

He bends his head to Edna and prepares to meet her lips.

'*Albert!*' The accusing cry comes from above. 'Albert Buckle, you come 'ere!'

They are all there, hanging over the railings of the Royal Hill, staring down at him: Mum, Dad, Aunt Ada, the kids, the Minchins.

'I'll not tell you again!' shouts Mrs Buckle. 'You just leave that little baggage be and come up here!'

'Didn't know it was the family shop you worked in,' Jack says scornfully.

'Oh, gawd!' Albert groans.

'Well, you'd better go to Mummy, then,' says Edna, and flings herself sobbing into Maisie's arms.

At that moment, Mr Seebold and his musicians strike up with 'Hold Your Hand Out, Naughty Boy!'

'Oh . . . *hell*!' says Albert.

Chapter 8

What with one thing and another, they get to the station only just in time. A lot of people seem to be making an early start for home this year, and a carriage can't be found with enough room for both the Buckles and the Minchins. They are just about to scramble into one, when Mr Buckle sees the fat man and his family already sitting there, and moves everybody on, saying loudly that he don't relish the company in there. To the impatient whistles of the guards and the slamming-to of doors, they just have time to find a compartment with enough seats for them all before the train pulls out.

When everyone is settled, Mr Buckle pulls fiercely at his pipe, and is soon immersed in the evening papers. He reads that German nationals resident in this country have been told to report to their embassy. He thinks of the quiet dignity of Charlie's rescuer. The wife is right: it must be rotten to be stuck in a foreign country when it's going to be at war with your homeland. He hopes he'll be all right.

Mrs Buckle nurses little Topsy. If they're all at Southend again next year, she should be walking. It's the first time Mrs Buckle has felt any doubt about a next year. She looks anxiously at her husband and her eldest son. Then Topsy belches and needs patting and her face wiped.

Aunt Ada sits nursing her grievances in silence. It crosses her mind that perhaps that German *pushed*

Charlie in. Well, of course, she isn't speaking now, but there'll come a time when she'll mention it.

Young Albert is even more sullen and laconic than his aunt. He still smarts from that humiliation. And, yes, he *will* join up, just as soon as he is able. You may have to take orders in the Army, but, at least, you are treated like a man.

Minnie, in between picking the heads off a bag of shrimps she has, stares at Florrie. She held her tongue all the time Mum was going on at Albert for kissing that girl, but one day she'll tell all right. It would surprise Aunt Ada to know how much her youngest niece takes after her.

Florrie felt very guilty when Albert was caught out, and she knows what is going on in that hateful little Minnie's mind, but she doesn't care. She thinks of the fat man's daughter, how pretty she is and how beautifully dressed. But she – Florrie Buckle – has been kissed by a boy on Southend Pier! She smiles contentedly.

And Charlie stands at the window as the train speeds through Chalkwell and Leigh. The sun still sparkles on the water, and some lucky kids are still playing on the beach. Then the last mast-heads disappear and Charlie sinks back into his seat. He wriggles uncomfortably in the damp swimming costume. Fancy falling in! For the first time he thinks about it and remembers the sensation of being swept under the jetty. If that man hadn't pulled him out, he'd have been drowned – everybody said so. He wouldn't be sitting in this carriage going home, he'd be ... Where would he be? He wonders who the man was. He ought to have said thank you . . . Still, it hasn't been a bad day. He has caught a fish. And there are still weeks and weeks before school starts again. There won't be any more seaside outings, but there's still lamp-post cricket, and rambles in Epping Forest, and no end of larks just mucking about, and . . . and . . . But, before the train has got to Pitsea, Charlie is asleep.

Historical Note

The following day, Tuesday, 4th August, 1914, Germany refused to withdraw her army from Belgium, and Britain declared a state of war. So began the Great War which lasted until November 11th, 1918. It cost the world millions of lives, and prepared the ground for the Second World War of 1939 - 1945.

The pier at Southend still stands. Sadly, the trains no longer run and the pierhead was severely damaged by fire in 1976. But, if you come and visit us, you can spend your day much as Charlie and his family did, for, although the Buckles are imaginary, everything else, you'll find, is real.

Other Titles in Andersen Young Readers' Library

Pamela Blackie — *Jinny the Witch Flies Over the House*

Roy Brown — *Chips and the Black Moth*
Chips and the River Rat
A Nag Called Wednesday

Frank Charles — *Beyond the Midnight Mountains*

Roger Collinson — *Get Lavinia Goodbody!*

Philip Curtis — *A Party for Lester*
Beware of the Brain Sharpeners
Mr Browser and the Brain Sharpeners
Mr Browser and the Comet Crisis
Mr Browser and the Mini-Meteorites
The Revenge of the Brain Sharpeners

Elfie Donnelly — *Odd Stockings*
So Long, Grandpa

Peter Hartling — *Theo Runs Away*

Geoffrey Hayes — *Patrick Comes to Puttyville*

Hans-Eric Hellberg — *The One-Eyed Bandits*

J. K. Hooper — *Kaspar and the Iron Poodle*

Christine Nostlinger	*Conrad*
	Lollipop
	Mr Bat's Great Invention
Jan Procházka	*The Carp*
Nora Rock	*Monkey's Perfect*
Brenda Sivers	*Biminy in Danger*
Angela Sommer-Bodenburg	*The Little Vampire*
	The Little Vampire Moves In
	The Little Vampire Takes a Trip
Robert Taylor	*The Dewin*
	The Line of Dunes
David Tinkler	*The Snoots Strike Back*
Hazel Townson	*Haunted Ivy*
	The Great Ice-Cream Crime
	The Shrieking Face
	The Siege of Cobb Street School
	The Speckled Panic
	The Vanishing Gran
Ursula Moray Williams	*Jeffy, the Burglar's Cat*
M. A. Wood	*Master Deor's Apprentice*

KS 2
20th Century Britain
1910's
First World War
World War 1